Handwritten note:
DEAR TERRI –
CONGRATULATIO
FOR CONTINUED SUCCESS!
(signature)

ENTRÉE Marketing^{SM}

Six Critical Principles
for the
Overworked Restaurateur

Mason Harris

Gazelles Publishing
Ashburn, Virginia

ENTRÉE Marketing[SM]:
Six Critical Principles for the Overworked Restaurateur
Copyright 2006 © by Mason Harris

This edition published by Gazelles Publishing. For information
contact Gazelles Publishing, Ashburn, VA.

For additional copies and discounts on bulk purchases contact
info@yougotmeals.com, or mharris@yougotmeals.com.

Design by Hallie Gladden, Ariana Patterson and Hugo Rivas.

First Edition

ISBN –10: 0-9765823-5-X
ISBN – 13: 978-0-9765823-5-9

Proudly printed in the United States of America.

10 9 8 7 6 5 4 3 2 1

"New Orleans food is as delicious
as the less criminal forms of sin."
Mark Twain - 1884

To the continued rebuilding of the City of New Orleans,
and the return of its people, character, and restaurants.

To my wife Robin.
Thank you for my greatest gifts -
your love and our two terrific kids,
Eric and Dana.

IN APPRECIATION

I've never written a book before. Trust me, it is much harder than writing 'Thank You' notes. I have written articles on various subjects, mostly related to restaurant marketing and diner loyalty, but the scope of this new effort was way beyond anything else I had attempted.

It could not have been written without the assistance of many people, some of whom I would like to personally and publicly thank right now. My primary editor, Jonathan Krasner, probably read and re-read this book more times than I did. Each time he found something of concern, like a punctuation mark out of place, an incorrectly spelled word, or a sentence that was incomprehensible, it required my attention. I finally had to stop him from reading so he could get back to his family.

My other valuable editors helped in so many ways, from corrections to fresh ideas. Bob Serber, Wendy Mackie, Jon Peacock, Harry Herskovitz, Ariana Patterson, Nick Gordon and Michael Birchenall, I thank you all for your contributions!

Verne Harnish encouraged me to step out of my safe world and write a book on restaurant marketing. Verne is the "Growth Guru" for thousands of businesses, founder of YEO, contributing editor for FORTUNE Small Business magazine, a terrific public speaker, and the author of 'Mastering the Rockefeller Habits – What You Must Do to Increase the Value of Your Fast-Growth Firm.' Without Verne, the desire to write this book would still be only a long-term goal. Partially as a result of his encouragement, it is now in your hands.

While I fit the researching and writing of this book into my daily work schedule, okay – maybe I missed more days or came in later than usual, my company still had to operate. These dedicated people kept us going and picked up my work: Jean Pierre Bassi Bikai, Andres Castro, Jose Corado, Neale Goodman, Adron Hawley, Andrew Hyatt, Avtandil Kobalava, Jonathan Krasner, Wendy Mackie, Kassandra Orozco, Ariana Patterson, Paul Pring, Hugo Rivas, Bob Serber, and Mark Singer. Thank you for your everyday and extra efforts!

There are many others who helped educate me, thereby contributing toward the ideas in this book. In no particular order, here are some of the people who deserve my thanks: Marcia Harris, Paula Kreuzburg, Rick Hendrie, Bill Brichta, Janet Broline, Gregory Schulson, Mike Wolf, Keith Watson, Bill Loukas, Rory Palmeri, Mike Sanford, Joe McCarthy, Steven Abdow, Jimmy Fragoyannis, John Laou, Larry Leonardi, Jeff Ecker, Don Noci, Jim Kohler, Bob Ansara, John Mayfield, Lynn Martins, Eric Lagrange, Mark DiMartino, Ron Fox, Dan Hudson, Russell Brown, Sam Facchini, Dan Lee, Hal Goldman, Mariko Hamada, Alan Hirsch, Hector Alvarez, Michael Smith, Pat Lee, Rusty Williams, Joe Gabriel, Licia Spinelli, Jackie Chin, Mary Ann Cricchio, Nate Garland, Brad Brennan, Paymon Raouf, Bruce Potter, Bernie Pankowski, Mark Leibman, Barb Simmons, Paul Hartgen, Lynne Breaux, Danny Mitchell, Michael Lattari, Bill Fultz, Crista LeGrand, Cal Clemons, Gina Rounsaville, and in memory of Marvin Price. (I am sorry if I missed you – let me know and you'll be in the next edition!)

I cannot finish expressing my appreciation without mentioning my parents, immigrants whose values and hopes for their children, have guided me through my journeys. In memory of my Dad, gone long ago but whose spirit is alive in my children, and in honor of my Mom who encourages me daily – thank you for your love and guidance. Oh, Mom – you can also tell the woman in Apartment 2-D that I may not be a doctor or a lawyer, but I am now an author.

ENTRÉE Marketing[SM]
Six Critical Principles
for the Overworked Restaurateur

Today's Menu

Starters

Entrees

ENTRÉE Marketing^{SM}

Chapter **1**

LET'S GET THIS
PRE-SHIFT MEETING UNDERWAY

October 12, 4:02 PM

"*Good afternoon everyone! Let's get started - we only have a few minutes for tonight's meeting and there's some important news to share.*

First, great job so far this month! Since making "increased appetizer sales" one of our quarterly objectives, appetizer revenue is already up 19% from the same period last quarter. The momentum from last quarter's focus, "increasing dessert sales," is continuing! Dessert sales were up over 16%. Most importantly – your average tips were up as well! See what a smile, some eye contact, a little "suggestive selling," and higher check totals do for us all!

Shilo, congratulations again – it's the second time this week you have led the group in "add on" sales and the highest check average. Thank you! (Robert and Ryan initiated the applause for Shilo.)

Second, the foundation we created months ago with the ENTRÉE Marketing^{SM} program is paying off. We're seeing more customers this quarter versus the same period last year, and some of you have expressed your joy, <u>and</u> exhaustion, at seeing a full restaurant this early in the week. The data and your fatter pockets (more tips) are proof of our progress!

A few of you noted that our base of "regulars" seems to be increasing – that is correct. Some of these customers are even asking to be waited on by specific servers. Do you think these loyal customers tip better? No more need be said about this correlation!

Let's remember the Principles in our ENTRÉE Marketing^{SM} program – we are creating the most loyal customers and friends in the city!

Any questions? Yes – Vanya.

"What are today's specials?"

Good question – thanks for reminding me. Everyone, don't forget to check the daily menu board in the kitchen for today's featured entrees; by the way, I loved the lamb and Paula told me the striped bass is fantastic!

Do not forget to tell your customers about the loyalty program via email – I expect three new customer sign-ups per server.

As usual, I will be on the floor as much as possible greeting our customers. Do not hesitate to contact me with any problems that you cannot solve, or to meet some first time patrons.

Oh, and Brian, tuck your shirt in. Okay - let's get started!"

PRE-SHIFT AS A METAPHOR

You can think of this book, and much of your business, as a pre-shift meeting. In this meeting, you are checking your progress, encouraging your staff, informing them of today's specials, solving problems, and aligning the team with your objectives.

In *ENTRÉE Marketing^{SM}: Six Critical Principles for the Overworked Restaurateur*, we will go through these steps, and much more. This book has been written to help every restaurateur, general manager, or anyone who dreams of owning and operating a restaurant, do a better job at marketing. Many of the concepts presented in this book came about through discussions with countless restaurant owners, your peers in the industry. ENTRÉE *Marketing^{SM}* was created to address the most common challenges faced by restaurateurs of all types, from independent entrepreneurs to managers of national chains.

As we did in this pre-shift meeting, we will start briefly with progress. You need to honestly evaluate the effectiveness of your marketing, particularly as it relates to your business objectives. Careful - overstating your success will leave you vulnerable to new and existing competition since you are assuming more loyalty than your customers probably feel. On the other hand, setting your marketing objectives too low, even if achieving them, also puts you at risk, as a better marketing program will lure your "occasional customers" away. All too often, significant customer loyalty frequently occurs accidentally, as opposed to by design.

Unlike the encouragement provided in a pre-shift meeting that is based on results, I am not in a position to give you feedback because I do not know where you started, how far you have come, and where you hope to go. You are in a great industry, but a very unforgiving business. You may have the finest wine selection in the city, but the upscale diner who feels slighted or ignored by your staff will find another fine dining restaurant, with a great wine list, to enjoy. If you are a "cheap eats" kind of restaurant, awareness of customer issues is also critical. Your local newspaper may have voted you as one of the "100 Best Bargain Restaurants," but your customer has 99 other Bargain Restaurants listed right in front of him.

> *You are in a great industry,*
> *but a very unforgiving business.*

In your world "today's specials" reflect varying availability of certain food items, their price, and even diet trends. Well, there are trends in marketing and advertising as well. Different media suit different size restaurants, at different times during their life cycles, and accomplish different marketing objectives. The point of this book is to help the committed restaurateur choose the correct marketing objective and the appropriate media at the right time, thereby resulting in a more loyal customer base and greater success.

In regard to problem solving, the fast-paced world of food service, with demanding customers, hot items served less than hot, and late food deliveries, does not support an environment for writing new operations manuals on a monthly basis. So we learn from our mistakes, correct them quickly (and permanently, if we are serious about success), and move on to the next customer.

The pre-shift meeting also serves to align everyone with the same goals. Your restaurant cannot succeed if there is a lack of clarity and commitment toward the goals, and alignment ensures that you are all "rowing in the same direction."

WHY FOCUS ON MARKETING?

Why are we concentrating so much on marketing? (I get that question a lot.) Let us think about what we would consider to be most important in a restaurant's success, based on our roles and training.

"People come here for my great food. I need to constantly improve the cuisine and menu," says the chef.

"If I can solve my personnel issues, and provide perfect service, we will be packed," says the General Manager.

"Given that I am now controlling food costs and expenses, we are more profitable than ever," says the Operations Manager (who may be the Chef *and* General Manager as well).

Let us not forget the customer, or take his loyalty for granted. "Where do you want to go for dinner tonight?"

asks an *occasional customer of yours*. "Let's go to the Olive Grove, they have the best crab cakes in Maryland!" *responds a loyal customer of theirs*. "Okay – the Olive Grove sounds good," says *your customer*. ("What? You are my customer – show some backbone!" you think as you look out at empty tables in your own restaurant.)

The Chef is right, as are the General Manager, Operations Manager, and everyone in your business who is focused on specific tasks. But ultimately, the most important "business partner and advisor" you have, the customer, chooses where to be fed, entertained, and psychologically rewarded for his decision.

> *Marketing is the separator.*

So why focus on marketing when there are other legitimate tasks that need attention? *Marketing is the separator.* Marketing encompasses the objectives of your Chef, General Manager, and the many employees who represent your restaurant to the outside world. Marketing done well, thoughtfully, and honestly, makes it easy for your customer, that necessary business partner and advisor, to choose you over and over.

Let me give you a personal example. Among the many fine steak restaurants in the Denver area, I ate at two of them, The Palm and Del Frisco, while in town on business.

Both restaurants are white tablecloth, fine dining, and comfortable. Service is typically exceptional and the food is high quality. If you are into wine in a big way, they have impressive wine storage areas. The wine is stored on its side, tilted slightly at the perfect angle to impress unsophisticated customers like me as to how valuable a wine collection it truly is.

The check average is relatively high; for me it is usually $65 - $80 for dinner. In some ways, the interior, food and service are similar enough that if you changed the sign on the front door and the logo on the menus, I might not be able to tell the difference. (I hope I have not offended the brand managers at both The Palm and Del Frisco with that last statement!)

Back to Denver – my meals at both restaurants were great, as was the service. The people I brought with me, and whose meals I paid for, were in agreement. In essence, both experiences were good enough for me to consider dining at either restaurant during a return trip to Denver.

As a matter of fact, in choosing between the two, I could just flip a coin for my decision.

Yet, on my next trip to Denver, one night only, I did not flip a coin. I consciously chose one restaurant over the other, without any hesitation.

Why? I just spent a page telling you how similar they were, and how the food and service were both great. Was it proximity to my hotel? No. How about price? No. A preference expressed by my dining companion? Sorry. I bet you will *never* guess.

It was marketing. *Marketing was the separator.* By the way, this specific marketing tactic was not expensive. It was not a TV commercial, radio jingle, billboard, or even a generous gift certificate (although that works very well for me too, by the way).

The reason I chose one restaurant over the other is because of something I considered remarkable. A few days after I returned home, as I was opening my mail, I noticed something unusual. Not "junk mail – this envelope is intended for recipients over the age of 21" unusual, but unusual because it had a Denver postmark. It was a handwritten "thank you" note from my waiter at The Palm. He had taken the time, possibly under the watchful eye of a very good General Manager, to write an out-of-town customer and invite him back.

I had never received a note like this from a server, so this marketing tactic was very effective. How effective? Not only have I been back to this Palm restaurant multiple times since, I have also told a handful of my friends, and tens of thousands of my readers, of this incident and how marketing makes a difference.

I know some of you are thinking to yourselves "Writing a thank-you note is not marketing. I am not sure what it is, other than a waiter with extra time on his hands, but marketing is advertising, or public relations, or coupons in the newspaper. It is what the big guys do to get people through their doors. What's worse, I cannot afford to market like that, so I will not even bother."

On the other side of the coin, some of you are thinking to yourselves "Okay, marketing is the "separator", but when everyone is doing the same things, how can I maintain my uniqueness? I can always come up with a new idea (or copy some competitor's idea, as long as he is out-of-state), but is there a framework or structure I can use to help me create a sensible, affordable, and effective marketing plan?"

This is a book for all of you. I am not promising it will change your lives, but I do promise that you will increase revenue and profits, generate ideas, think more creatively, implement sound training procedures, and strengthen your brand in the customer's mind relative to the competition. All you have to do is overcome your inertia, your "we've always done business this way" mindset, and implement the principles you will learn.

Now tuck your shirt in, and let's get started.

"One morning, as I went to the freezer door, I asked my wife, 'What should I take out for dinner?' Without a moment's hesitation, she replied, 'Me.'"

Anonymous

Chapter 2

TOP NINE EXCUSES FOR FAILURE

January 6, 9:59 AM (about 9 months earlier)

*E*ric hesitated before walking into the office, extended his hand and stepped forward.

"Hi Mr. Adams, it's good to see you again. I hope you and your family enjoyed the holidays. Were you busy?"

"Good to see you, Eric. We did enjoy the holidays, thank you. We're really not that busy at the bank during the week between Christmas and New Year's, so I was able to take the family to see some relatives in New York," responded Jordan Adams, *the bank's Senior Loan Manager. "Now Eric, I know you wanted to speak with me about increasing your line of credit. Is that right?"*

"Yes, that's right Mr. Adams, and I appreciate your seeing me on such short notice. I've brought my financials for the last calendar year. The holiday season wasn't as profitable for us as we had hoped.

You know, the rain and bad weather kept people indoors instead of eating out, and with gas prices so high, people didn't have as much discretionary income available for restaurants," responded Eric. "You know my restaurant, Fish Outta Water, has some very loyal customers, and I know we will bounce back this quarter. Plus – we just got a good write-up in a local paper! Of course, I had to advertise with the guy to get the write-up, but at least he spelled our name right!"

Jordan hesitated before responding and studied Eric. He liked Eric, respected his entrepreneurial spirit, and knew he was a talented chef. But Jordan was worried for Eric. Despite 70-hour workweeks, Eric's restaurant just was not growing, and in actuality, the profits seemed to be diminishing even though revenue was starting to stabilize.

"Eric, you have maxed out your term loan on equipment and renovations, and now your line of credit is fully used. I am worried about what could happen to you if you do not turn your restaurant around. Tell me honestly – what are the problems you are facing?"

"Well Mr. Adams, we have our troubles, but there isn't anything I cannot overcome. Anyway, here are the biggest issues I am facing."

Two hours later, Jordan Adams made up his mind. Eric seemed to be honest and hardworking, but he wasn't getting any more money from the bank today. And he had better develop a workable action plan very quickly.

The economy can feel like a roller coaster, and few industries respond to every bump and turn like the restaurant industry. Wages increase or taxes are lowered and consumers have more disposable income for optional items, like restaurants, new vehicles, extra vacations, and 22' fishing boats.

Inflation outpaces real earnings or taxes are increased and consumers brown bag it to the office. Through it all, good times and bad, some restaurants thrive and others go under, frequently replaced by a new restaurant concept in the same location.

One might suspect that since we are experiencing record restaurant industry sales (projected over $500 billion in 2006), and sales growth for the last 14 straight years, that the biggest problem most restaurateurs face is how to spend their wildly escalating incomes.

Approximately 925,000 restaurants are operating in the U.S., giving credence to advice from Hollywood: *"If you build it, they will come." (Field of Dreams 1989)*

Success is not automatic. Maintaining a thriving restaurant, as external and internal factors change around you constantly, is a serious challenge. There are numerous reasons why you *might* fail, but when identified, we can develop strategies to succeed despite the obstacles.

EXCUSE # 1: TOO MUCH COMPETITION

(About two hours earlier:)

"Mr. Adams, there is just too much competition in my county. Frederick County has a population of just over 215,000. If you look at the Yellow Pages Directory, you'll find more than 400 restaurants listed! There are 34 pages with restaurant names, phone numbers, addresses, and menus! Of course we are in there so our customers can find us, but every time I turn around, it seems like a new restaurant is opening up!

I even paid to be listed on the County's tourism web site. That's only 274 restaurants and someone has to scroll though about 10 pages just to find me," stated Eric.

"Quantity of competing restaurants," wrote Jordan Adams in his notebook under the heading *'Fish Outta Water.'*

The restaurant industry is growing. A growing industry with bright prospects for the future attracts new entrants. Get used to it.

The Tortilla Factory in Herndon, Virginia, celebrated its 29th Anniversary this year. When they first opened up, it was the only restaurant for many miles. Today, you can walk out the door of The Tortilla Factory, turn right or left, walk 10 minutes, and pass 10 restaurants.

Despite the competition, The Tortilla Factory is still a favorite of the changing local community, and some of its customers will drive from Maryland, 20+ miles away, to enjoy the food and atmosphere.

EXCUSE # 2: TOO MUCH *CHAIN* COMPETITION

"And it is not just the number of competitors that worries me. Every time one of those national chain restaurants opens up, they advertise like crazy and become a $2 million a year location overnight! And to add insult to injury, some of my servers leave me and work for them." Eric was looking depressed.

"One time after work when I pulled into my neighborhood I saw my next door neighbor, a good friend, and he had a bag from California Pizza Kitchen. I tell you; even their take-out bags are nicer than mine!"

Jordan Adams wrote, "Chain restaurant expansion, cool take-out bags," in the notebook.

It is true that the opening of a national chain near one's own independent or chain restaurant may induce shortness of breath, occasional headaches, and remorse over not having gone to law school instead.

A national chain restaurant in your area may do other things that affect you as well. It can bring more people who have never tried your restaurant close by, giving you an opportunity to attract them. For many of these dining consumers, this may be your best opportunity to get on their radar screen.

You may be forced to examine your strengths and correct your weaknesses. Have you been taking your "regulars" for granted? Now may be a very good time to express your appreciation to them and reward them for their loyalty. They will most likely check out the chain restaurant and become a "regular" of theirs as well. You need to ensure that some other restaurant, chain or independent, loses the customer's dining dollar. You can still maintain your share of her dining and entertainment choices.

EXCUSE # 3: NOT ENOUGH TIME

"I am working longer and harder than I ever have before, yet I cannot seem to get the important daily tasks finished. Seven days a week, 10 hours a day – I need more time!

It starts with food delivery in the morning, although we also pick up some items locally a few days a week. Before you know it, lunch is approaching and at least one day a week, one of the servers is late or doesn't even show up.

Then we're cleaning up, meeting with vendors, and preparing for dinner. We need to verify inventory and schedules, and we'll check the reservations in our system. Of course, if the weather turns bad, that hurts us too!" Eric continued, "Do you have any aspirin?"

"What about marketing, server training, financial reviews, employee meetings, and licensing requirements?" asked Jordan as he wrote some more in his notebook.

"Well, we handle these issues when we have time...and more time is something I cannot buy yet from a supplier."

Even if he could find the time, there's a good chance it would not be used to address those new issues. There is an old adage that goes something like this: "The amount of time needed to complete a project expands to fill the amount of time, plus extensions, *available* to finish that project."

Frankly, technological innovations are making restaurants more productive. Increased productivity means restaurateurs do have time for more things, or may even be able to work shorter weeks!

Your POS systems are computerized, allowing you to more quickly and accurately communicate a customer's order to the kitchen. Quicker service can mean faster table turns and higher revenue within the same physical facility. More revenue without the expansion and construction costs – we all like that!

The Internet, email, and online ordering from suppliers allow you to accomplish more in less time. Fewer and shorter vendor meetings enable you to spend more time training employees, planning, implementing effective marketing tactics, and meeting customers, as soon as you decide those are important enough issues.

EXCUSE # 4: NO BUDGET

"Maybe I'm doing something wrong with my budgeting process, but since I try to follow the budget as closely as possible, I am constantly unable to

*implement programs I think would benefit me. I
would like to try some new marketing programs, add
some more order-entry terminals, or even renovate
the restrooms, but the budget just does not allow for
it.*

*Fortunately, I seem to be under budget in total
employee training, compensation, and benefits." Eric
looked hopefully at Jordan and waited for some
approval, but it never came.*

Too many restaurateurs fall back on their "budget" as
a reason to dismiss something new and potentially
valuable. We all want to improve but if we do not have
enough information to feel comfortable, or are too lazy to
learn more, we are typically reluctant to make the necessary
investment.

Think of your budget as a road map. You use the
map to plot a course to a destination. Some elements are
truly fixed, like a critical bridge that you must cross. For
example, you cannot stop lease payments for the kitchen
equipment you purchased. These fixed elements do not
change easily and they are simple to identify and specify.

Other items in our budget, our road map, provide
flexibility. We can choose to make some detours on a trip
because these detours will enhance the experience, or
because some roads are no longer attractive options due to
construction. Within our restaurant budget, we can choose
to invest in a better marketing program if we see that it
generates traffic sufficient to justify additional outlays. We
are over budget on the line item for marketing, but we are
also over our profit forecasts because of the marketing
program that we successfully implemented.

What situation would you prefer: a more profitable restaurant or a pat on the back for not exceeding your expense budget?

This is not advice to disregard your budget, especially if it was well thought out and reviewed. It is recognition that your budget is not a set of handcuffs that limit your ability to make decisions in a constantly changing environment.

EXCUSE # 5: STUCK IN A BAD LOCATION

Eric continued, "I also wish I wasn't stuck in this location. It's not bad, but it is certainly not as good as some new neighborhoods being built. But I have so much invested in the construction, furniture, atmosphere and lighting fixtures that to move would really set me back. Not to mention the years I still have remaining on my lease.

Also, if I moved, I would have to create a whole new base of customers. Some of them might follow me to this new location, but I am sure that most of them will not even know where I moved!"

The location you choose prior to opening your restaurant is one of the most critical marketing decisions you will make. Current population and demographics, trends in the neighborhood, both residential and commercial, as well as expected development will undoubtedly impact your success.

Once you have made your decision and opened up, excluding any catastrophe, such as what the residents and businesses experienced in New Orleans with Hurricane Katrina, you can be successful.

You will have to modify your menu and maybe even your format to reflect changing trends and demographics. You will need to reexamine your marketing plans to ensure they are properly targeted and that you are not overpaying.

Although the location does contribute toward your success or failure, it rarely determines it. You can most likely think of numerous restaurants that have failed in great locations, only to be replaced by other restaurants that have succeeded. You can probably identify restaurants that have survived and thrived in the same location for 30+ years, even as the neighborhood changed dramatically around them. And finally, every dining consumer I know can tell you about the "really great restaurant that no one knows about because it is off the beaten track." If no one knows about it, why is there still a wait to get in for dinner?

If you love steak and you are in New York City, visit the original Peter Luger Steak House in Brooklyn. Opened in 1887 (that's right, you read it correctly, almost 120 years ago!), this neighborhood has seen some changes. Yet somehow Peter Luger still does a thriving business despite significant neighborhood changes, what many might politely refer to as an "undesirable" location, and the ever-increasing quantity of very fine steak restaurants in New York City. No excuses for Peter Luger, just exceptional product, service, and marketing.

EXCUSE # 6: UNMOTIVATED AND UNDEPENDABLE EMPLOYEES

The doodles on Jordan Adams's notepad were now getting larger and more detailed.

"Some of my employees are just driving me crazy. Don't they understand that if the restaurant does well, they share in the success?

Let me give you an example. I just cannot motivate them to "sell" desserts and coffee to diners after the meal. I know with certainty that some of my customers finish their entree and then walk down the street to a little bakery with tables for after-dinner dessert and coffee. I know these customers would enjoy our desserts – we have a great pastry chef! We only use premium, imported coffee. Is it so hard to suggest dessert and even bring some samples over on a tray to show and entice our customers? Higher checks lead to increased tips for them, too!

Oh – and by the way, these are my better employees. The bad ones call in an hour after their shift has started to tell me they'll be late, or can't even come in. I end up waiting tables instead of managing the kitchen and handling problems!"

One critical factor that determine your success or failure, if not the most critical factor, is the "face" your customers see when they dine with you. Your customers do not know how efficiently your kitchen operates, how clean it is, or how involved you are with the community.

But the "face" that they experience and draw their perceptions from belongs to your employees. If your hostess has a strong odor of cigarette smoke on her clothes, this leaves an impression on your customers, whether or not they are smokers.

If your servers are unfamiliar with your menu, slow, or unenthusiastic, then the great food, wine list, and location are not prominent in your customer's mind when he leaves. The indifferent attitude of your staff is what makes him exclude you from his dining choices in the near future.

Hiring correctly, regular and ongoing training above and beyond what your competition provides, and daily pre-shift meetings all help to keep your staff aligned with your core values.

EXCUSE # 7: CUSTOMERS COULDN'T RECOGNIZE QUALITY FOOD AND SERVICE IF IT SMACKED THEM IN THE HEAD

"Let me tell you, we serve the finest food in the city. I only buy the best ingredients possible – this is not an area to cut corners! I know that my cost of food as a percentage of revenue is higher than the industry average, and it's due to the better quality I start with every day," Eric explained.

"Unfortunately, too many customers do not appreciate the difference! All our fish is truly fresh. It's caught and served in our restaurant within 48 hours, and usually within 24 hours. We get a lot of our fresh fish from local markets less than 2 hours away!

We do not have a lot of beef on the menu, but our steaks are premium aged, not the lower cuts of beef our competition serves.

People would prefer our food if they were eating at home, yet here they do not appreciate the quality.

Sometimes I think I need a better class of customers to be successful!"

"So now it is the customer's fault," Jordan thought while nodding his head.

Every restaurateur I have ever met, when pressed, has confided that he has some customers he would not mind losing to his competition. Actually, many of these restaurateurs might even think about anonymously mailing these troublesome customers a coupon to the competition with the hope that they take their business elsewhere.

We all know the type of dining customer I am writing about. These customers mistreat your staff with rude remarks, complain loudly and frequently about your food and service, send multiple entrees back, leave a minimal tip, and probably take two parking spaces on a busy night.

Unfortunately, there is very little you can do. Treating any customer rudely will bounce back and hurt you badly. As much fun as it is for a customer to share with friends a really exceptional experience at a restaurant, it pales in comparison with the pure joy of ensuring a truly miserable restaurant experience is spread to every one he has ever met in his lifetime, and even to some people who are complete strangers. This "I'll teach them for treating me badly!" approach is part of our genetic code, an emotional revenge with some psychological reward and no perceived downside.

A large, national consumer electronics store took an interesting approach to a problem they had with a small percentage of their customers that abused the return policy. Some of their customers were purchasing expensive equipment, like computers or video cameras and returning it for a full refund about a week later. It seems some of the customers were using these consumer electronic items as a free test-drive to get them through an important college paper or vacation. Some of them would return to the store a day or two later and buy back the equipment at a significant discount, as this equipment was no longer brand new, and was now offered on a "clearance table."

So this company changed their return policy to prevent this type of abuse. Restocking fees, shorter return periods, returns for store credit only, and even identifying the abusive customers internally to prevent the next purchase from occurring were implemented, even at the risk of alienating some better customers.

The result: increased profits for this chain as many of the offensive customers took their business elsewhere.

You undoubtedly have customers like these, people who take advantage of your good nature. I wish there was an easy way to identify them and politely ask them not to come back, but I do not know how to tell you to do this, nor am I comfortable that you should do this. The danger for some restaurateurs is the ease in which we can blame lousy customers for problems, even when the lousy customer problem is of our own making. It should not be a surprise that lousy operations and poor food and service will increase your percentage of disgruntled customers! Your own operational issues have become the "cause" and the only "natural" effect is an increasing base of irritated and angry customers.

So before we start refusing service to a percentage of our customers, those identified as "customers from hell," we need to be sure they cannot be converted into some of our best friends and a source of new diners anxious to try us because of the positive word-of-mouth they keep hearing!

EXCUSE # 8: CHANGING DEMOGRAPHICS

"Before I bought this restaurant I used to actually come here with my friends for a good evening out. If I had a special date, this is where we went.

It had everything – a great bar when we waited for our table, fun staff, exceptional food – this was one of my favorite restaurants. The place was always crowded.

I think the neighborhood has really changed a lot, and people living near here now are not that interested in our fare and atmosphere.

Mr. Adams, I am sure some of your other clients are experiencing the same problem," stated Eric. *"Even your bank must have a very different mix of commercial and personal banking clients."*

"It is true the neighborhood has changed over the years," responded Jordan, *"but this branch has grown each of the last five years."*

Some neighborhoods change over time, creating new challenges for all of their businesses. Changing income levels, education, type of households, and ethnicity will affect the success of your restaurant – unless you are effectively attracting your new neighbors.

Restaurants that have become icons have always intrigued me. Not because of a very quick rise to fame and popularity, but because of their longevity. Sometimes these are family restaurants passed from one generation to the next. Other times the new owners recognized some assets that are hard to value, including the charm, neighborhood appeal, and customer loyalty included in the purchase price.

Seibel's, in Burtonsville, Maryland, is a great example. Founded in 1939 as a "dairy bar" it began producing premium ice cream (this was when "premium" really meant something). Breakfast, lunch, and dinner were added to the menu over time.

In 1971, after thirty-two years of establishing itself as the finest and friendliest restaurant in the county, an employee purchased the restaurant from the Seibel family. Thirty-five years later, Seibel's is still thriving even as the surrounding community grows and new restaurants seem to open every few months.

From dirt roads and horse drawn wagons, families now arrive at Seibel's for great American food in their SUVs and station wagons. Oh – and the ice cream is still premium; handmade the way it was sixty-seven years ago, when the neighborhood demographics were different than they are today.

EXCUSE # 9: BURDENSOME GOVERNMENT REGULATIONS

Jordan Adams checked his watch and turned to Eric. "I'll submit the paperwork and we will call -"

"Speaking of paperwork," Eric interrupted, "do you know how hard it is to own a restaurant nowadays simply because of government interference? Of course, we should be subject to reasonable regulation and oversight since we serve food to the public daily. But it seems like every time a politician is up for reelection and needs some publicity, some new regulation harmful to restaurants is proposed!

I can live with the important stuff. It takes time for me to send employees for food handling and safety certification. And we also have to regularly train our staff with regard to serving alcohol; particularly in regard to ensuring the customer is of legal age and isn't carrying the latest fake ID sold on the Internet.

The worst intrusions we are now facing include a non-smoking ban throughout the County, new labeling on our menus that are expensive and cumbersome, mandatory health insurance coverage for all employees, and higher wages for entry-level employees. I spend half a day each week just trying to make sure we are in compliance with every rule and regulation."

Yes – our industry is heavily regulated, and at some level, unappreciated. We contribute significantly to the economy at the local, state, and national level. We provide tremendous opportunities for employment and advancement into management, as well as opportunities for entrepreneurs to open their own restaurant or buy into a national franchise.

However, it is the requirements above and beyond food handling, employee tax withholding, and the sale of alcohol to adults that are troubling. Too often legislation affecting restaurants is considered or implemented without consideration of the financial and operational impact on a restaurateur, its employees, or customers.

Special meal taxes, tourist taxes and license requirements are easy ways for politicians to help cover budget shortfalls.

The threat of "obesity lawsuits" still hovers for some restaurants, particularly if they are perceived to have "big pockets" available for settlements. Multiple lawsuits have been filed against restaurants. McDonald's won a victory when one lawsuit was dismissed, but other cases are pending.

Even if the primary targets right now are large restaurant corporations, eventually insurance companies will add some of this increased risk to their business policies for the small independent restaurants, at a higher cost.

Anti-smoking fanatics have had success in banning smoking in restaurants across various states. A restaurateur can be fined because a smoker lights up, despite the numerous "Non-Smoking" signs that have been added to the restaurant. (I am not a smoker, and as a consumer I would prefer a non-smoking restaurant when dining out with my family. However, until smoking becomes illegal, I am opposed to banning it in private businesses.)

OVERCOMING EXCUSES

The common excuses I hear from restaurateurs can be overcome. Some problems are simple to solve and corrections can be made quickly. Other issues take planning, agreement from your staff, and well-executed implementation.

Typically, these excuses, or business problems, fall into one of three categories: 1) external issues, such as competition and changing demographics, 2) internal issues, such as employee motivation and retention problems, and 3) organizational issues, such as time management and budget difficulties.

As you will see, marketing done well minimizes, or even eliminates, some of these headaches. We will let your competition complain about their problems; keep reading and you will learn how to solve yours.

"...steam was generated beyond the power of the canister to endure. As a natural consequence, the canister burst, the dead turkey sprang from his coffin of tinplate and killed the cook forthwith."

News report of an industry accident (1852)

Chapter **3**

APPRECIATED? NO...
HOW ABOUT INVISIBLE?

January 15, 12:23 PM

" *S* *orry about the wait,"* Dana apologized to *her lunch companions Samantha, Pauline and Nathalie as they were seated. "They do not take reservations. I hope we still have time to go over everything during lunch.*

What's worse, I was here in the mall about 11:35 to return some items and wanted to put my name in for our 12:00 lunch, but they wouldn't take it! They said I could be seated immediately, but if I came back in 15 minutes I would have to wait in line with everyone else. This person is new I think, because they have taken my name before in this same situation!

Once I am in the restaurant, what is so hard about taking my name for seating so I can run an errand in the mall first? They put names on a list when there's a line anyway. This chain is getting too popular!

It is so frustrating! As often as I eat here, you would think they could show me some consideration. After she told me she wouldn't take my name for later, she looked right past me at the next person in line! You know - I like the varied menu and the food is pretty good, but I need to find someplace else for these lunch meetings."

This chapter is not really about reservation policies, lunch meetings, or greeters in your restaurant who need to be better problem solvers.

It is about making a customer feel small, unappreciated, unimportant, and irrelevant. (You know, kind of like dealing with the IRS, but with less fear.) As consumers, we can easily feel that our business is next to meaningless to most restaurants, especially if it is a location grossing over $1 million a year.

If we think long enough about it, we may even feel a touch resentful when we conclude that our frequent visits and loyalty to a specific restaurant are little more than data points on some manager's desk. Gross sales, check averages, gross margin, average party size and number of desserts – they are all necessary for monitoring progress, making decisions, and printing those colorful graphs. But the trend turns downward when customers begin to feel invisible.

There is a category of your customers known as "regulars"; you know their faces and may even know some of their names. They never feel ignored because even in the event of some problem with service or food, they are confident you will be there for them and make it right.

Even when everything is perfect, they derive extra satisfaction because of the handshake, eye contact or greeting they receive from you or your staff.

They provide a steady revenue stream for you and are very likely to introduce new customers to your restaurant. Thank you, oh loyal "regulars."

Chances are these regulars are a small percentage of your patrons. It is clearly valuable but also impossible to get to know the many customers who pass through your doors and receive your hospitality every day. Unfortunately, too many restaurateurs do not even try. Hence, the "invisible diner" syndrome occurs, and like the "Invisible Man" horror movies of old, be careful. It is hard to defend yourself against something you do not see.

> *Your "regulars" are a small percentage of your patrons, but your "invisible customers" provide the greatest opportunities for growth.*

IF SOMEONE TREATED YOU THIS WAY, YOU WOULDN'T COME BACK EITHER

It does not have to be rude behavior that causes customers to become "ex-customers", or even just "not-as-frequent customers." Fortunately, rude behavior is rare in the restaurant world. (Actually, it is rare when someone in the hospitality industry is rude, but not as rare when it is the customer exhibiting offensive behavior.)

The problem for you is simple. Although you try hard to provide good food and service to your customers, all that does is make you the *equivalent* of every other good restaurateur within 10 miles of your location. When you and the great bulk of your competitors succeed in "raising the bar" related to food and service quality, the consumer clearly benefits...wherever she goes! So what are you doing to make her choose you more often? What have you done to ensure that she does not feel "invisible," just one of many patrons?

Let me give you a real-life illustration.

I eat out regularly, 1-2 times a week for breakfast, 4-5 times a week for lunch, and 2-3 times a week for dinner, for a total of 7-10 meals per week. (This does not include my morning coffee stop, 4-6 times a week, where the competition within 3 miles of where I work includes, Starbucks, Dunkin Donuts, 7-11, Vie de France, and other take-out, convenience store, and various quick-stop locations.)

Without even including morning coffee stops, I eat out 7 –10 times a week, or 350 – 500 times a year. I guess this means I should be a very desirable customer to you.

	# Per Week	Annual
Morning Coffee	4 – 6	208 – 312
Breakfast	1 – 2	52 – 104
Lunch	4 – 5	208 – 260
Dinner	2 – 3	104 – 156
Total:	11 – 16	572 - 832

An analysis of my restaurant choices, created by examining credit card statements and estimating the non-credit card eatery visits, identifies some interesting, but not unexpected, patterns. (The following data does not include meals paid for by cash, or by someone else. The restaurants listed on my credit cards represent 50% - 70% of my estimated meals outside the home.)

Although I live in the Washington DC metropolitan area, which encompasses the District of Columbia, Maryland, and Virginia, I ate in 10 other states during the previous 12 months. The out-of-state restaurant visits were related to both business and personal travel.

Out of 253 restaurants identified on my credit card statements, 222 were in DC, MD or VA, and 210 of those were within 15 miles of my home or office.

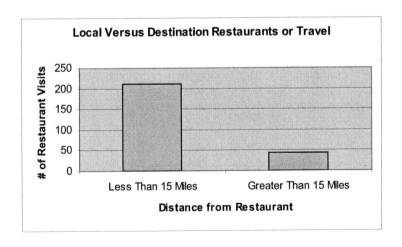

Our first obvious conclusion: *since 83% of the restaurants that I visited (and paid by credit card) were within 15 miles of my home or office, your marketing*

efforts need to be targeted to consumers within this range, or even less.

Some restaurant consultants will encourage you to limit your advertising to people within 15 minutes, not miles, of your restaurant. Your effective reach may now be as little as 5 miles.

The only exception is a "destination" restaurant. Do not make the mistake of assuming that a specialty dish or two makes you a destination restaurant, because it will lead you into making bad marketing decisions. Restaurants waste a great deal of money marketing to people beyond the natural limit of their true reach. We tend to go to neighborhood restaurants for typical fare. The definition of "local" differs around the country. Someone living in the densely populated upper West Side of Manhattan might consider a local restaurant to be one that is within 1 mile, or 20 city blocks. A resident of Wyoming may consider a local restaurant to be anything within 30 miles.

IT'S CALLED PAYBACK

My 253 meals were spread among 102 different physical restaurants. The number of different brands represented was 86, as some chain restaurants were visited across different locations. Although more and more fast food and quick service restaurants are accepting credit cards, all of these 86 restaurant brands were full service, ranging from an average check of $10 - $80.

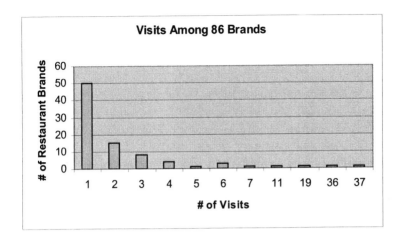

Of the 86 different restaurant brands identified, I visited only 13 of them (15%) 4 or more times during a twelve-month period. The remaining 73 brands were visited 3 or fewer times, as follows: 8 of the restaurants (9%) were visited 3 times, 15 of the restaurants (17%) were visited 2 times, and the remaining 50 restaurants (58%) generated a single visit.

Our second obvious conclusion: *I like to try different restaurants, 86 to be exact, giving them a chance to earn my loyalty. But they have to make a very good impression to deserve a second or third visit.* Only 13 of these 86 brands (15% of restaurants) accounted for 59% of my total visits. These restaurants were visited at least once per quarter on average, and as often as every 10 days. If we define a "regular" customer as one who visits at least 6 times per year, only 8 of these restaurant brands (less than 10% of the total) can consider me a regular customer. These 8 restaurants accounted for virtually half of my total restaurant visits.

If you owned or managed one of the 65 restaurants that hosted me once or twice, would the experience you provide be enough to turn me from an occasional customer into a more frequent diner?

Can we assume that there were fundamental problems with the food, service, or atmosphere at those restaurants that failed to earn return business? The answer is definitively "no."

Was the food on par with prison cuisine? Do the servers need training in how to be less surly? It would help so much if these were just bad restaurants! Then we could explain it away!

> *Reaching out to your customers, recognizing them, making them feel valued – these are the critical 'personal touches' that are lacking in too many restaurants. Is yours one of those restaurants?*

The food and service were probably average to good. If you ask me why I do not frequent a specific restaurant more regularly, it is likely that I just do not think of it very often. As well, if I do not think of a restaurant, I cannot recommend it when someone asks me where he or she should dine. Now expand this failure to a great many more customers, none of whom are recommending a specific restaurant that is okay but forgettable, and you begin to understand why word-of-mouth is nonexistent, making new customers hard to attract.

Why do I, and frankly too many of your customers, visit your restaurant less frequently than you would hope?

It's called "payback time." As a result of my feeling invisible to you, you have become invisible to me. Welcome to your own personal "Twilight Zone."

"Always serve too much hot fudge sauce on hot fudge sundaes. It makes people overjoyed, and puts them in your debt."

Judith Olney

Chapter 4

MARKETING TRENDS:
EMBRACE OR EXPIRE

January 19, 8:13 PM

*D*ana finally returned home from dinner, this time at one of her favorite Mexican restaurants. The restaurant is reasonably priced, serves consistently great tasting food, and she had the attention of her server, Paul, from the moment she sat down. During the meal the restaurant's manager, Margaret, stopped at her table to ensure that she was enjoying her food. "No wonder it's so popular," she thought.

She still had work to do, however. Dana was giving a marketing presentation to a bank client's small business customers the next morning and needed to refine some of her slides. Although she had given this presentation, or a similar one, many times before, she knew that it should be updated constantly to reflect reality.

"Marketing is never static," she reflected, "and not recognizing trends leads to bad decisions. I will add some material to the presentation based on items

*I have read this week. Then, if I have time, I'll check
my email and watch some TV. "*

MEDIA FRAGMENTATION

In the "old" days, marketing was much easier,
especially if you were a big company with a large budget
for mass media advertising. Your preferred advertising
choices were TV, followed by more TV, and if absolutely
necessary, radio.

Why was mass media so effective? It drew
tremendous audiences.

Let us look at data for the series finales of some of
our favorite TV shows: Friends, Seinfeld, Cheers and
M*A*S*H. Start by guessing which of these shows
correlate to the number of viewers in the chart below.

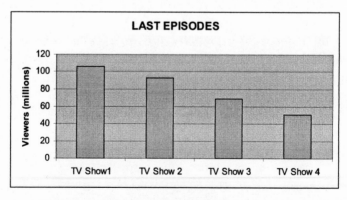

Now let us check your answers.

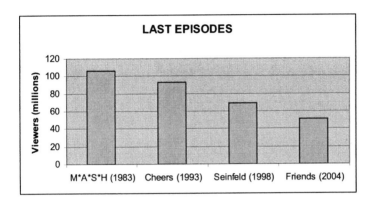

Did you get these shows in the correct order from the most viewers to the least viewers? Congratulations – but you probably watch too much TV. Try to get more exercise.

These are the four highest-ranking "last episodes" in TV history. From 1983 (M*A*S*H with 106 million viewers) to 2004 (Friends with 51 million viewers) there is a decline in viewers of the top-ranked series finales in excess of 50%.

Our population did not decrease by 50%; it actually increased by 59 million people between 1983 and 2004. So what happened?

Something else increased significantly: we gained more TV channels and more entertainment options. Lots more options.

These options, including hundreds of TV channels (versus a half dozen channels), pay-per-view (versus watching what the networks broadcast on their schedule), the Internet, and more, have created challenges for the marketing professional.

Since a great deal of advertising is based on reaching and impacting a customer while she is being entertained or otherwise engrossed in something of interest, like a favorite TV show, radio station, magazine, web site, or newspaper, the advertiser (you!) needs to be more selective in the media options you choose.

There are so many options to choose from today, it leads to confusion, wasted resources, frustration, and failed marketing efforts.

New magazine titles, targeted at very specific readers are on the rise. Cable TV viewers are increasing at the expense of network TV. Daily newspaper circulation is down for the umpteenth year in a row as every major newspaper provides access to their articles on the web.

Let us use a different analogy. About 10 years ago, your sub shop was one of three restaurants in the neighborhood, the other options being pizza and a nicer full-service family style restaurant. Today, you are one of fourteen options on "restaurant row" and your competition includes Chinese, Mexican, Indian, Sushi, Italian, Steak, and Seafood restaurants, ranging from quick serve, to fast casual, to table service, to fine dining. This restaurant "clutter" is analogous to marketing "clutter."

If "media fragmentation" is starting to give you a headache, take some aspirin and calm down. For most restaurateurs, although there are many marketing and advertising choices, only a few are really necessary in your marketing plan. We will explore these later.

CLUTTER

You and each of your customers were exposed to over 1,000,000 advertising messages and brands last year. This equates to over 2,700 messages per day, roughly 170 messages per waking hour. Thankfully, the advertising community cannot inundate us with ads while we are sleeping (yet).

It is not just TV, radio, billboards and print media that are flooding us with ads. These images, logos and labels attack us from coffee cups, storefronts, clothes, the Internet, and more.

I cannot process these ad messages; there are just too many. Frankly, I can barely remember to pick up the kids after tennis lessons once a week.

Fortunately for all of us, our brains block the great majority of these messages. Only a fraction of them get through and the messages that have some impact on us will change over time depending upon various factors, most important of which is our perceived need for a product or service at that moment.

With all these attempts from hundreds of companies to motivate our purchasing behavior, from shopping to dining, we have a significant challenge ahead of us. With so much clutter attacking our senses as consumers, it is easy to spend our limited marketing resources incorrectly as businesspeople. How can we grab the attention of a dining customer and influence his decision to eat at our restaurant instead of a competitor who is equally accessible and attractive?

Think of clutter as a buffet table overloaded with similar food options. Most diners will fill up their plates with things they know they enjoy, sample some new items, and ignore the rest. (This analogy does not, of course, apply to the Midnight Buffet on any cruise ship, where everything, including linens, is eaten.) When it comes to advertising, consumers will take in the ads that are immediately relevant to them, remember some ads that are particularly creative and may have some future relevance, and ignore the rest.

Breaking through the clutter is necessary or your marketing and advertising will have the impact of a Diet Coke at the cruise ship buffet.

LIFESTYLE ISSUES

People are living longer due to medical advances. More single parent households, both male and female, are in existence today than ever before. The divorce rate seems to be in a never-ending spiral upwards. Income, age, education, marital status, race, religion, and partner preference are among the many lifestyle choices and/or demographics that influence purchasing and dining preferences.

Your restaurant may appeal to a specific consumer profile, or your customer base may be varied. You would not try to appeal to high-income individuals for your fine dining, $75 per person dinner the same way another restaurateur will attract customers looking for quick service burgers, chicken, or tacos.

That seems pretty obvious. So why are so many restaurateurs "hunting" for customers using the same media that their competitors use? Why haven't many restaurateurs changed their marketing approaches to reflect the lifestyle choices of their customers?

There are many reasons – none good. Inertia. Laziness. That is the way it has always been done. Lack of knowledge. The part-time waiter is taking a marketing course and he created the marketing plan.

Let us start with understanding how important generational marketing can be. We know that age is an important factor in customer buying decisions, and even the ability to purchase.

My teenage son may have developed an affinity for good steak restaurants because our family dines together on special occasions at Morton's, The Palm, Ruth's Chris, the Capital Grille, Fleming's, or a fine independent, Jordan's. You can market to him all you want, but unless it is his birthday, he is not choosing the restaurant.

More sophisticated restaurateurs are moving away from mass marketing, the "create an ad for everyone" approach, toward more individualized marketing that concentrates on more personal needs. Income and education are characteristics we can use to create more individualized ads, but equally important is age. You can reach a great many people in specific age groups with appropriate ads that are relevant and personal, but you initially need to understand how to identify these groups.

GENERATIONAL MARKETING

Marketers have segmented the generations into four primary groups, based on their year of birth. The shared cultural experiences of the people in these groups differ from the other groups, and marketing efforts need to reflect these differences.

"The Greatest Generation": This group consists of those Americans born prior to 1945, and they encompass roughly 21% of the population. World War II and the development of nuclear weapons uniquely influenced them. Saving for the future because of uncertainty about the economy and national security was paramount, especially because they experienced shortages, rationing and the Cold War. This hard working generation is typically conservative in their spending habits. We joke about the "Early Bird Special" for diners in this category, because it is accurate. Although certainly not everyone in this generation eats dinner at 4:30 PM, most of your customers who take advantage of the "Early Bird Specials" are in this generation.

"Baby Boomers": were born between 1946 and 1964. This is the largest of the generational groups we serve today, and it represents roughly 32% of the population. Boomers are critically important to family and fine dining restaurants. This generation grew up in an expanding economy, where many former "luxury" items became commonplace and expected. Educational and employment opportunities were abundant, and this generation prospered and became wealthier than any previous generation. Typically spoiled by their parents who wanted a better life for their children following World War II, this generation broke many of the social norms embraced by their parents and introduced major cultural changes during the 1960's and 1970's. Although defining themselves as more liberal in their politics, unlike their conservative parents, this generation is becoming more conservative as they approach retirement.

"Generation X-ers": The Gen X-ers were born between 1965 and 1980, after the high growth rates of the Boomer generation ended. Comprising roughly 18% of the population, this generation is equally comfortable in quick-service restaurants and fine dining restaurants. Born just after the introduction of the birth control pill in 1960, during the height of the Civil Rights movement, or after the Supreme Court's decision on Roe versus Wade which legalized abortion in 1973, this generation grew up in a time of rapid social change and divide. They witnessed the fall of the Soviet empire and an economic roller coaster, including the boom and bust of the "dot com" era. This generation is well educated, but many have not done as well as their parents. Their trust level of corporations and government is low, and many expect that Social Security benefits will be reduced as they approach retirement.

"Millennials": This generation consists of those Americans born after 1980, and is the fastest growing generation, currently 29% of the population. Need help with your home computer? Ask a Millennial! This generation has experienced rapid technological changes since birth. Divorce, single parent families, and joined families, are as normal as watching video footage of military conflicts on the Internet. Access to information and the ability to find answers to questions they would never ask their parents can be obtained by querying their favorite search engine. This generation loves its fast food and fast casual restaurants. Service with a smile has been replaced by service with a smile and multiple body piercings.

Certainly there are those born in these generations whose upbringing and values are different than the rest of their generation, and the typical characteristics described will not fit everyone. As well, the sizeable immigrant community, including the first generation born in America, may share considerably different characteristics.

From a marketing standpoint, understanding that certain groups, be they generational, income, education, or religious, share experiences and motivations. As a restaurateur, you will find greater success in modifying your marketing strategy to both contact and meet the needs of those groups most important to your success.

TECHNOLOGY

Changing technology affects our marketing success in many ways. Technology enables us to better target our customers and prospects, at a lower cost.

Let us start with how we get our news. For the generations prior to the Millennials, newspapers and TV were the primary news sources, as well as major advertising vehicles. We saw earlier how media fragmentation has eroded the number of viewers of network TV. A similar downward spiral has occurred for daily newspapers. As an industry, daily newspaper circulation has declined for the last 17 years, and there is no reason to believe that this is ending.

Technology in the form of the Internet is becoming a major, if not the primary source of news, for many of your customers today.

Technology in the form of Tivo and its digital video recorder competitors enables users to bypass commercials. I can watch a one-hour prime time show in about 48 minutes. I have been told that I cannot buy more time. But it seems that technology is enabling me to do more things that I want to do, without being interrupted by commercial messages for products that have no appeal to me, *in less time*. That is not a bad option for me, but it is a nightmare for advertisers.

Do you remember when a phone was just a phone? My current cell phone takes digital pictures, shoots video clips, provides me a calendar for appointments, maintains my contact directory, browses the Internet, retrieves and sends emails, plays songs, interfaces with my Bluetooth enabled automobile, creates text documents and spreadsheets, entertains me with games, downloads videos, sends text messages, synchronizes with my home and office computers, reminds me of tasks, tells me what time it is anywhere in the world, and will soon broadcast TV shows. Oh – it also makes and receives calls.

If this "phone" was more attractive and could cook, the divorce rate would take a major jump again.

MEDIA INDUSTRY CONSOLIDATION

There was a time when businesses implementing their media plans made several calls to different companies. Depending upon the company's size and media budget, all or some of these media outlets would be contacted. A local radio station focused on playing oldies from the 80's. A local TV station affiliated with a major network would be called to book available spots on the Oprah show. A local billboard company would be called about availability on some key roads in proximity to the customer. The phone company would be called about placing an ad in next year's Yellow Pages directory. The big-city newspaper would be called about rates for an upcoming special section.

If during your conversation with the sales representative for these media outlets you felt the rates were too high, you had options. Pick a different TV station and get a show that reaches similar demographics. Choose a different radio station and format. If you really wanted to leverage your power, you might threaten to move all the money you had budgeted for TV into billboards, radio, and newspapers. That usually helped move the negotiation forward, or at least got you more advertising for less money.

Media consolidation has changed that dynamic. Giant media companies today own several of the media outlets. A multi-billion dollar company may now own the same radio station that you worked with before. This company also owns multiple radio stations in the same market, as well as TV stations, newspapers, billboards, and it has a major Internet presence.

Although only a small minority of restaurants should even consider TV or mass media in their media mix, the example is still important. If you do a lot of print advertising, larger conglomerates are purchasing many smaller newspapers. The end result includes increasing rates, less negotiating power, and reduced competition for your advertising dollars.

There are advantages and disadvantages due to these consolidations. Bottom line, however, you need to understand who your customers are, how they can be reached, and how to measure the effectiveness of your marketing.

Or you can do what many restaurateurs unfortunately do – give up on sensible marketing and pray exclusively for good word-of-mouth.

"I'm at the age where food has taken the place of sex in my life. In fact, I've just had a mirror put over my kitchen table."

Rodney Dangerfield

Chapter 5

ENTREE MARKETING: SIX CRITICAL PRINCIPLES

January 20, 11:29 AM

*D*ana's presentation on Small Business Marketing was well received by the bank's clients and some of the audience members were still waiting to speak with her before leaving. She pleasantly greeted and spoke in turn with each attendee who had patiently waited to meet her.

Dana understood one rule of marketing very well, which so many others seemed to ignore. "Serve your customer's customer." She provided marketing services to her client, the bank, and it was her idea to give these "Small Business Marketing" presentations to the bank's customers. The attendees felt the information and ideas they obtained were well worth the hour or two away from the office, and they appreciated their bank's efforts in providing this non-traditional benefit.

From the bank's standpoint, keeping and attracting new commercial banking customers can be expensive, and sometimes the answer lies in providing valuable non-banking benefits along with the same financial products every bank offers.

As a side benefit, Dana sometimes found that an attendee of her presentation became a client as well.

Finally, the last person in the room approached her, hand outstretched, and introduced himself. "Hi, I am Eric Nathans and I am with 'Fish Outta Water', the best seafood restaurant in the city. That was a great presentation you just gave"

"Dana Nichols," she responded, shaking Eric's hand. "I am pleased to meet you, and I thank you for your kind feedback! What do you do at the restaurant?"

"Well Ms. Nichols, I am a trained chef. I hire, train and manage the employees. I deal with our vendors and the many organizations requesting free gift certificates for their fund-raising activities. And I have personally guaranteed all the bank loans, leading to many sleepless nights," responded Eric.

"You sound very busy, and please call me Dana. The "Ms. Nichols" stuff is making me feel old."

"Okay Dana, I would like to invite you to lunch at my restaurant. I forgot to mention that I am also in charge of marketing, and I honestly do not think I am doing a good job bringing in customers. My food is great, my servers are really trying, but my marketing efforts are not working. I need help and after today's presentation, I am hoping you are the person who

can make the difference with my marketing. Will you help me?"

"I am not sure. We will have to see just how "great" your food really is," responded Dana, with a smile.

What is ENTRÉE Marketing^{SM}?

en-tree *n.* 1. a. The main course of an ordinary meal. b. A dish served in formal dining immediately before the main course or between any two principal courses. 2. a. The power, permission, or liberty to enter; admittance. b. Access by special privilege to a place normally inaccessible.

In the restaurant trade, when we hear the word "entrée", we first think of our menu items. Entrees are typically the highlight of the meals we serve – and they frequently leave the strongest impression on your customers. No one cares how good the salad was if the entrée was bad.

Way back in our high school English class we learned that entrée also means access and admittance, frequently to places where access is not usually granted.

ENTRÉE Marketing^{SM} is a series of marketing and business principles (because marketing *is* business) that will give you access to your customer's loyalty. Loyalty is not easily earned, or readily accessible. Loyalty requires an investment, but it is priceless. Seth Godin, one of the best marketing gurus alive, goes further. In his book "Permission Marketing" he describes the need to "turn an occasional customer into a friend." Friends have loyalty; occasional customers have many, many options.

The restaurant industry is unique in many ways. There is no other industry that has so many "occasional customers", all of whom can become your friend with the proper efforts, leading to an astronomical increase in their revenue contribution to your restaurant. Friends love to share, and these "occasional customers" who have become loyal friends, your *best* dining customers, will communicate their superb experiences at your restaurant with *their* friends. It is word of mouth, personal and electronic, taken to its highest level, and you are the beneficiary.

> **Friends have loyalty; occasional customers have many, many options.**

ENTRÉE Marketing[SM] for restaurants starts with this fundamental realization: you can increase your revenue and profits more quickly and economically by motivating existing, occasional customers to increase their frequency. Too many restaurateurs have prioritized the goal of obtaining new customers. Customer retention and increasing existing customer visits are frequently secondary goals. Borrowing again from Seth Godin, you need to spend more time "farming" your assets, and less time "hunting" for new customers.

Farming is done inside your four walls, on your premises, and with permission-based communications to your customers after they have left the restaurant.

Do you remember the data from Chapter 2 detailing my restaurant visits over the course of a year? My credit card receipts identified 86 different restaurant brands (over 250 total restaurants) where I dined.

Most of these restaurants made an effort to ensure my visits were pleasant, and they sincerely believed that good food and service would bring me (and the bulk of their customers) back consistently.

It is such a shame that their good efforts do not ensure success. Out of the 86 different restaurant brands that benefited from my visits, how many do you think made any effort to reach out to me after I had left? How many invited me back for a special occasion, like a birthday or anniversary? How many sent me a personalized direct mail letter or email to thank me? How many attempted to reward me and motivate me to return again within a specified period of time?

You can count the number of those restaurants on the fingers of one hand.

> Out of the 86 different restaurant brands that benefited from my visits, how many do you think made any effort to reach out to me after I had left? How many invited me back for a special occasion, like a birthday or anniversary?

That is why we need help with our marketing. There are six primary principles of ENTRÉE Marketing^{SM}, one for each of the letters E – N – T – R – E – E.

1) E: Entice your customers to return. What does the first principle teach us? We will learn how to create a warm, welcoming, and attractive environment inside your restaurant. This atmosphere creates positive experiences for customers, be they loyal friends or first-time diners.

After learning how to "farm" inside our four walls, where does ENTRÉE Marketing^{SM} take us next? Well, we stay inside those four walls, but turn our attention to the most critical factor influencing your success: your workforce.

2) N: Near-perfect service is achievable with the right people. Recruiting, testing, training, motivating, keeping (and "losing" certain people when appropriate) quality employees are critical requirements for your success. You need to pay as much attention to these tasks as you do to visits from health department inspectors. I am very serious. Be honest with yourself. Intellectually you know how necessary exceptional employees are to your success, but too often you "settle" for what you have. (I can feel your heads shaking in agreement as you read this.)

All too often, the really great efforts you make in your food selection, choices, preparation, and presentation can be overshadowed by the minimum wage employees, inadequately trained, who interact with your dining customers from the moment they enter your restaurant (earlier if you have valet parking) to the moment they leave.

3) T: Top-of-mind is the position you want in your customers' minds. Advertising strategies to reach appropriate targets, including existing friends (since you are converting occasional customers into friends), and the most appropriate new potential customers, are the foundation for the next principle. You want your customers to think of you first when choosing a restaurant.

With so much competition and advertising clutter as barriers to establishing that special awareness with customers, you need to understand which advertising options move you toward your goals, and which options are the equivalent of burning $20 bills as a fuel source in the kitchen.

4) R: Rewards are a basic human motivator. This next principle examines human motivation and how our decisions are influenced. Other companies are motivating you to purchase their products and services. We can learn from them and implement a reward system that makes your customers feel special.

From airlines to grocery stores, elementary schools to Fortune 100 corporations, and almost everything in between, some bright manager, teacher, employer, parent, or restaurateur has already discovered the unquestioned value of "compensating" his customer. Compensation can be tangible or emotional, convenience or currency, but it is an important differentiator between you and your competition.

5) E: Eighty / Twenty Rule can be used to your advantage. Postulated over 100 years ago, ENTRÉE

Marketing's next principle was introduced to the world by Vilfredo Pareto, an Italian sociologist and economist. His theory demonstrates how a small percentage of effort, resources, people, and ideas result in a disproportionately higher level of success.

The corollary of this powerful insight is the awareness that the majority of your problems, challenges and disappointments are the result of the same small percentage of poor decisions, personnel, and marketing errors. If you can identify, focus on, implement, and manage the "critical few", your successes will come more easily and your biggest problems will become more manageable.

6) E: Email marketing is a tool for reaching those who are critical to your success. This final principle is the key to ensuring that an appropriate level of your marketing efforts is truly effective, relevant, personal, and desired by your most important customers.

You will not have to worry about ad clutter interfering with your message. Your communication will not annoy and interrupt your customer as he is busy with something else. These marketing efforts will become more easily measurable, in regard to both customer response and increased revenue.

It works with one restaurant location or thousands of locations.

In the Washington DC area, the Clyde's Restaurant Group has earned a first-rate name for itself. From the opening of its first location in the early 1960's, it currently owns twelve truly unique restaurants. There is no cookie-cutter approach in the development of a new Clyde's restaurant. Independent and very successful, its restaurants cater to the local population, visitors, and the powerful politicians who have made DC their second home.

Through a variety of carefully selected media that encompasses local newspapers, limited radio spots, and an email program, they reach existing and prospective customers regularly. Exceptional staff and food, served in impressive settings, along with talented and forward thinking management, shows how embodiment of the right principles leads to distinguished success.

Numerous restaurants have implemented programs to increase revenue and loyalty. Now it is your turn – let *ENTRÉE Marketing*[SM] *for Restaurants: Six Critical Principles for the Overworked Restaurateur* be your roadmap for increased loyalty and success.

"You better cut the pizza in four pieces because I'm not hungry enough to eat six."

Yogi Berra, Baseball Player

Chapter 6

'E' ?
ENTICE YOUR CUSTOMERS

January 20, 1:34 PM

*D*ana sipped on her coffee and reflected on both her meal and her potential new client, Fish Outta Water. As she looked around the dining room she thought of her other restaurant clients and how she had helped them with their marketing struggles.

She had already identified areas of improvement for Eric to work on, just from this first lunch. Too many questions about Eric's marketing remained to be answered, but she was confident she could help make Fish Outta Water a bigger success.

"I was correct, wasn't I? This is the best seafood restaurant in the city!" Eric moved into the chair across from Dana's. "Would you like some more coffee?"

"Yes, thank you, I would love another cup."

Eric looked around for Dana's waiter to get some more coffee but couldn't see him, so he went to refill the coffee cup himself. He returned to the table with fresh cups of coffee for them both.

"Okay, the truth. What did you think of the meal? Don't spare my feelings!" smiled Eric.

"The salmon was very good and it was presented nicely on the plate. The salad was crisp and fresh, and this coffee is excellent."

"I knew I had something special here, I bet this downturn is temporary," responded Eric, pleased with this evaluation.

"Well - do not bet too much just yet, you have other problems that need to be corrected. I suspect people enjoy your food but do not become repeat customers for some very important reasons." Dana studied Eric's face and waited for a response.

He thought about what he had just heard. Finally, he asked Dana, "Can you please be more specific?"

"Sure – you are missing the first two essentials of the ENTRÉE Marketing^{SM} system, that's obvious. The remaining principles I don't know about yet, but I can learn after meeting with your staff and you." Dana looked at Eric and continued. "Eric, I know I can help you. We would both benefit if you became my client and I was able to show you how to fill your tables. I can start my work this week; trust me, you need me to start as soon as possible."

Eric smiled weakly. "I'm not sure I can afford you – we haven't talked about price. I do not even think I have enough in the budget for a new marketing program. Maybe I should think about it. Plus, I never even heard of the ENTRÉE Marketing^{SM} program."

"Eric, you can't afford <u>not</u> to make some changes soon, whether with me or with someone else. Let me prove my value. I will go through the first principle with you now, and then you can decide whether or not to hire me." Dana put her napkin on the table. "But you are buying my lunch regardless."

Eric laughed. "It's a deal. Give me a few minutes to find the waiter and refresh our coffee."

Design Your Restaurant to Entice

En-tice: *v.* To attract by arousing hope or desire; lure.

Diners frequently remark on a restaurant's "atmosphere," its "ambiance," and its "character." Many restaurateurs pay for expensive designers and architects to ensure that this elusive objective, creating an "enticing" atmosphere is achieved.

During a presentation a restaurateur once asked me if "enticing a customer" really matters. "People come to a restaurant to satisfy a need. They're hungry, they need to eat, and then get back to their lives. I am conveniently located so they come to me."

Enticing your customers is critical, unless if you have a captive market, leaving them no choice but to put up with you. Some people believe they have a "captive" market, but the only true instance I have seen is the dining room at a prison.

Many factors contribute toward an enticing restaurant, and you will still be successful even if you do not possess them all. However, the more ways your restaurant entices people to return frequently and recommend you to their friends, the more successful you will be.

Following are those factors that most contribute toward "enticement":

Food Taste

Taste is subjective and the same dish may have a diverse appeal to different diners. However, when preparation and quality remain consistent, people who develop a liking for your food will judge the taste based on their prior visits. If the taste is dramatically different, possibly because a different chef created it, new ingredients were substituted, or the dish sat undisturbed under a heat lamp for too long, you risk being on a roller coaster of customer opinions.

We strive to first make the food taste as good as possible and then need to ensure it is consistently prepared. How important is consistency? It helped create one of the best-known brands in the world.

Many people may not think that McDonald's Big Mac is the best tasting burger around, but they consume it as if it were. Why? Ray Kroc, McDonald's founder, aside from being a perfectionist in regard to so many elements of his stores, understood that a Big Mac in New York needed to taste exactly like a Big Mac in Texas. It is a result of strict food preparation and guidelines. (Of course, local and regional preferences will account for different menu options.) The family stopping after four hours on the road for dinner is not in the mood for surprises when it comes to feeding their hungry kids.

Food that consistently tastes the same frequently becomes "good" or "acceptable" to your diners. If they do not like the taste, they will find another option. Hopefully it will be a different entrée on your menu; the worrisome situation is when it is an entrée in a different restaurant entirely.

Menu Design, Table Settings and Server Uniforms

Your menu is your corporate brochure. Would you buy from a company whose brochure had multiple incorrectly spelled products, was stained with food, and made you feel like washing your hands immediately after putting it down? (Sign on menu: "All employees must wash hands after touching the menu.")

Your menu should be neatly printed and easy to read. Poor lighting and small, fancy fonts make me take out my reading glasses so I can decide what to eat. Thanks for making me feel old. (Whether I am old or not is irrelevant if I have to struggle to read your menu. I was with someone at a dinner once who had so much trouble reading her menu she held it too close to the candle for extra light. The resulting fire made it much easier for me to read my menu.)

If you are a quick service restaurant and the menu items are displayed on a menu board behind the cashier, consider having paper menus available as well. This enables customers who have difficulty reading menu boards from a distance to place orders more quickly when they reach the counter.

Just as your menus need to be readable, the same applies to your menu boards. I recently visited a national chain known for their fresh breads, sandwiches, soups and salads, and had difficulty reading the beautifully designed menu boards because of the italic font and small lettering.

Daily menus imply fresh food. Daily specials accomplish the same objective, albeit for fewer items. Even if you have a well-designed printed menu, ensure that the specials are nicely printed and attached to the main menu, assuming you are not counting on the server to correctly remember the specials.

Table settings – the proper flatware and glassware accompanied by a napkin, ought to be simple. Instinctively, there should not be too many ways to mess this up.

So why does it happen so frequently? How does improperly cleaned flatware end up on a table? Bad dishwashing followed by an employee who is not paying attention when setting the table. There are few things that turn off a diner more that food residue on his fork, clear fingerprints on her knife, or lipstick on his coffee cup (well, most guys at least).

Missing flatware on a table are sometimes the result of an uncaring staff, but other times occur because a diner at the next table, having dropped his fork on the floor, simply takes one from an adjoining table. Your staff has to be aware of the table settings because from the customer's standpoint, whatever the reason, incomplete and unclean sets leave a negative impression.

Server uniforms are an important part of the "image" you are creating for your restaurant. Start with nametags, they are effective and they help create a bond if your customer bothers to address a server by her name. The lack of a uniform can fit your image as well, but that should be the intention. There is room to be creative with server attire. If you operate a sports bar, servers can wear different sports uniforms depending on the season. During football season, it would be fun to have servers with their names (or nicknames) on the back of the uniform along with the restaurant name and logo. These should be worn on game days. Put your busboys in referee shirts. The same goes for your local hockey and basketball teams. You do not have to wear their uniforms; create your own uniforms for each of the sports.

If you have a Mexican restaurant, you can go with sombreros or fake mustaches every once in a while. Create a fun atmosphere that is memorable and remarkable. It gets people talking and coming back.

Presentation

Whether the food handed to your dining customer comes wrapped in silver foil, or is on fine china nicer than most people have in their own homes, is a reflection of the people you are trying to attract and serve, not as much the food you prepare. Both Mamma Lucia and Vince & Dominic's, two fine but very different Maryland-based restaurants, serve pizza, essentially made from primarily the same ingredients, and both great tasting. One restaurant, a quick-serve independent, serves its pizza on paper plates and sells them by the slice. The other restaurant, an excellent family casual, full-service, growing regional chain, uses tableware appropriate to its extensive entrée offerings. Both present the same basic product, pizza, appropriately for their clientele.

Most consumers become more aware of the food presentation when they dine in fine dining restaurants. Higher dinner prices and restaurants selected for their ability to "impress" generate different expectations from consumers. If you neglect to meet these expectations, you risk failing to make your restaurant enticing to that customer in the future, as the need to impress a business associate or date is never-ending.

Greeting Area, Waiting Area, and Bar Area

Your customers relax, communicate with friends, and eat at your tables, whether they are manufactured from shiny plastic built to withstand the strongest and most out-of-control toddler, or fine wood designed to impress adults.

But they wait *somewhere* in your restaurant for that table. For most people, it is a short wait at the Greeting or Reception Area. Designed to direct your customer's attention once they have entered your restaurant, it serves as the staging area to locate tables and seat your patrons. Aside from possibly a coat-check area, this area is the first opportunity you have to welcome customers back or greet new customers. Unfortunately, for some restaurants, the "welcoming" and "greeting" parts seem to have been overlooked. In its place, I too often see staff that is tired from standing for so many hours, bored during slow periods, and frantic during peak dining times, yet barely proficient at saying much beyond "How many in your party?" and "Would you like crayons with the kids menu?"

It hurts – this is a lost opportunity for you! You can rise above the competition by asking for names and if these customers are returning or if this is their first visit. The purpose in asking is not to make pleasant conversation; it is so that your Manager on Duty can approach each table at some point during the meal with advance knowledge about the diner.

I am accustomed to being seated, ordering, eating, paying, and leaving (most of the time in that order). It is rare that I am approached by anyone other than my server asking how my meal is. It is even more unusual when I am approached by a manager, welcomed back or thanked for trying the restaurant for the first time. It is extremely atypical – but it has happened! – when this same manager encourages me to visit again soon and hands me his business card with a handwritten note on the back offering me a "specialty appetizer" as a reward next time I come in.

Which of these above scenarios would be enticing to you for a repeat visit, especially if this was your first time at a new restaurant?

I recommend asking these questions at the greeting area before your customers are seated, as opposed to at the table. When you determine this right away, the information can be subtly communicated to your staff through a variety of methods. For example, it can be noted on your table chart to alert the manager, or by the placement of a different flower vase at the table when your customers are seated. You may have three variations of the flower vase, or three different flowers, signifying returning customer, new customer, and a mix.

Most restaurants use a "name" to identify the party being seated. On a few occasions the hostess asked for my name and that of my dinner companion prior to seating us and passed this information to the server. She used our names in addressing us, and we then bothered to learn her name. Without a doubt this affected our perception of the service and restaurant, and of course led to a higher tip for the server.

Waiting Area - If you have a busy restaurant, your Waiting Area is crucial. We are not living in a culture that is "patience" oriented, particularly as it relates to eating out. Waiting in line at the Department of Motor Vehicles, at a checkout counter in the grocery store, or for a table in your restaurant, are all activities we prefer avoiding. Frankly, our culture competes on the speedy delivery of pizza, and this delivery time occurs more quickly than some police responses! So if you are fortunate enough that your restaurant's popularity leads to high demand and some wait time for patrons throughout the week, do not let that become a negative for you!

Make sure the waiting area is comfortable and heated or cooled as necessary. Many of your customers will wear their outer garments in a waiting area and take them off when they are seated. This might require a different temperature setting. Have a server pass through your waiting area with mini-appetizer samplers. Your guests will appreciate your consideration, they will be more likely to wait instead of going across the street to a competitor, and they undoubtedly are more likely to return because they have been treated so well!

Bar Area – This area, if you have one, is part of the impression you leave with your customers. Although some of your patrons are coming specifically for the bar, others are in the bar only as long as it takes to get their table. These people should not feel pressured to order drinks, or they may feel their "waiting time" is artificial, and your purpose is to drive revenue through alcohol sales prior to the meal.

Cleanliness and Rest Rooms

There is no such thing as "too clean" in a restaurant. I have never read a restaurant review that complained about glassware that "sparkled too brightly," "floors that were so spotless you could eat off of them," or "servers whose uniforms were so clean and pressed they distracted from the otherwise enjoyable biker bar atmosphere."

Clean without obtrusive is the objective. How can a commitment to cleanliness be construed as obtrusive? You do not want to have a strong disinfectant odor anywhere, even in the rest rooms.

And speaking of restrooms, if you have not already purchased the automatic flushers, get them installed as quickly as you can. If you have to, barter gift certificates for your food with an independent plumber, but do not put it off any longer. I cannot overemphasize the importance of restroom cleanliness. Too many restaurants fail in this area, do not be one of them.

In regard to hand dryers, I suggest you offer dryers as well as paper towels (or cotton towels if you are fine dining). These options cover the environmentalists as well as those who never cared for trees. If you install a hand dryer, make sure it is properly maintained. I was in a restaurant restroom once and used the dryer after washing my hands. It was powerful, which was good, but so loud it sounded like an airplane engine. My hands were dry but I could not hear the waitress when I got back to my table.

Lighting, Sound, and Artwork

Decisions in regard to these contributors to (or detractors from) your brand identity require careful consideration as well.

Lighting can be used to create an atmosphere that is dreamy or elegant, or it can accentuate the table setting, artwork, and furnishings. Bright lighting implies clean and well maintained, but would diminish the mood for a starry-eyed couple desirous of a candle-lit romantic dinner with wine.

The food you serve, the clientele you seek, and the image you wish to build or maintain should help you identify your lighting needs. Most customers of quick service restaurants go there for convenience, speed and price. These customers are not expecting, and would even be surprised, if the lighting created a mood more appropriate to a restaurant on top of the tallest building in the city.

More than light, sound can inadvertently become a detractor inside your restaurant. This includes the sound of many diners speaking loudly to each other, and the music played throughout the restaurant to maintain an atmosphere appropriate with the brand.

The excitement of a loud, bustling restaurant is attractive to many diners, but is potentially a turnoff to diners in the Greatest Generation, and even many from the Boomer Generation. If your target market includes customers from the Generation X-ers or the Millenials, a loud, active, and youthful atmosphere is appropriate.

Artwork and wall decorations, range from posters, and oil paintings, to plasma TV screens, and need also be appropriate to your food and clientele. At some level this is obvious but it is amazing how many restaurants seem to get this wrong anyway. Fortunately, except in fine dining, this mistake is not as costly in terms of leaving customers with a negative feeling, as might happen with poor sound or lighting.

Brand Image

I have referred on multiple occasions to your "brand image" and its importance.

You may consciously strive to create a brand image that people will identify with your restaurant. This can be strengthened with many of the specific actions necessary to make your restaurant enticing. If you do not have a clear brand message that you are trying to get across, the market will fill one in for you, and it may not be what you want.

Customers associate images and feelings with brands, and these feelings strongly influence purchasing (and dining) decisions.

Let us try to illustrate this with a little test. Pick three adjectives for each of these consumers: 1) People who drink Starbucks coffee, and 2) People who drink 7-11 coffee.

Adjectives such as successful, wealthy, highly educated, and sophisticated are more frequently associated with the Starbucks consumer.

Starbucks has created a brand that is the "affordable luxury" to just about everyone. Sure, the coffee may cost a dollar or two more, but who does not think he is worth it? We all prefer drinking or dining where people with similar interests dine. (Or consumers we *would like to identify with* go for their coffee.)

We may never own or drive a Rolls Royce, but we all get to reward ourselves with the Rolls Royce of coffees.

You may not want to be the Rolls Royce of enchiladas. That is okay; there are so many unique ways to position your restaurant among customers and prospects. You might prefer instead to be the Nordstrom's of your foodservice niche. You can choose authenticity as the brand image for your Italian restaurant. Just choose – and then support your brand image and associate it with positive thoughts in your customers' minds so that they can be enticed back more frequently.

> ➢ What are you currently doing to entice existing customers to return?
> ➢ What can you change to become more enticing?
> ➢ What can you do to entice new customers to try your restaurant?
> ➢ Can you entice your loyal customers to bring their friends and refer you more frequently?
> ➢ What would be the cost of making your restaurant more enticing versus the benefit of increased business?

"Tomatoes and oregano make it Italian;
wine and tarragon make it French.
Sour cream makes it Russian;
lemon and cinnamon make it Greek.
Soy sauce makes it Chinese;
garlic makes it good."
         Alice May Brock (Alice's Restaurant)

Chapter 7

'N' ?
NEAR-PERFECT SERVICE
BRINGS THEM BACK

January 27, 6:34 PM

*D*ana and Eric had been seated about a minute when chips and salsa were placed on their table. They had waited in the bar area at the Rio Grande Café for roughly 10 minutes and Eric was impressed with everything he had seen so far. "It's Monday night and they have a full restaurant. Not bad," he thought a little enviously. His own casual full service restaurant was typically slow on Monday evenings, and he had left his GM in charge tonight.

Following Dana's presentation on "Enticing Your Customers" Eric was suitably impressed with her marketing knowledge and hired her to get his marketing focused. Today was lesson number 2, and Dana would not tell him the topic. She wanted him to experience "one of her favorite restaurants" as a customer.

Dana took one of the tortilla chips, dipped it into the salsa and put it in her mouth. "You know how some foods you just cannot stop eating after you have started?" she asked Eric. "These chips and salsa are too good – I cannot exert much control here so please make sure that when they offer us a second basket, you say 'no'!"

Eric smiled and tasted a chip as well. It was good, and definitely not from a bag.

The waiter approached, waited for a break in their conversation, and introduced himself. He took their drink orders and asked if they had previously dined at Rio Grande. Upon learning that Dana was a regular and Eric a first-timer, he welcomed them and promised a great evening of food and attention. He concluded by reciting the day's "specials," asked if they had any questions (they did not) and went to get their drinks.

A few minutes later he was back and he placed the drinks on the table, first by Dana and then by Eric. "Would you like to order now or do you need a few more minutes?" he asked.

"I think I'm ready," said Eric, but Dana was still considering the many entrees.

"Please take your time; I'll be back again soon to check with you. Would you like another basket of chips and more salsa?" he asked, eyeing the half-empty basket on the table.

"No," replied Dana immediately, "but I am ready to order now."

They placed their orders and the waiter left.

"Okay – we've covered the first ENTRÉE Marketing^SM principle, an "enticing" experience that brings people back. So what is the next of your ENTRÉE Marketing^SM principles?" Eric asked Dana.

She started answering just as their waiter returned with drink refills for them both.

Perfect Service is Impossible –
Near-Perfect Service is Achievable

serv-ice: *n.* 1) Work done for others as an occupation. 2) The serving of food or the manner in which it is served.

I have never met a successful restaurateur who did not list "good service" among the top three contributors to his or her success.

Most restaurants provide "good" service, or what should be more appropriately described as "acceptable" service.

An acceptable level of service is not bad, and it keeps you in the game. Obviously, no restaurant can survive with a culture of bad service; the problem occurs when individual servers are not aligned with the restaurant's true service objectives, and their less-than-sunny dispositions or mediocre work ethic poisons the dining experiences of your customers one day at a time. We all know that one bad incident can lose you a valued customer, and customers tend to share the "bad" faster than the "good" experiences. Truly bad service is a fundamental sin in our service-oriented industry.

Perfect service is a wonderful goal but very rarely achieved. Proper recruiting, testing, motivating and training will consistently lead to "near-perfect service" and that puts you head and shoulders above the great majority of your competition, who have learned to live with, and even embrace, merely "good service."

I read of a survey that asked major corporations if they provided "superior" customer service. A large majority, 80% of the surveyed companies, replied that their service was superior.

The same survey organization asked these companies' customers if they were receiving "superior" customer service. A significant minority, 8% of the customers, felt the service was superior.

This is what many in the business community refer to as a "disconnect".

We fool ourselves into believing that our service is exceptional and consistent, our staff members feel as strongly committed as we are, and that our customers would agree with our (incorrect) self-assessment. It is time for a reality check because improving service levels and consistently providing "near-perfect service" will contribute greatly toward higher revenues and profits in the long-term, more so than changing your menu or implementing short-term promotions and marketing plans.

Recruiting

Everyone you hire is an ambassador for your restaurant. It is not just your servers or greeters. Your busboys, dishwashers and line chefs have friends and family, and like most of us meet new people frequently.

How often does this question arise when meeting someone new? "So, what do you do for a living?"

Which of these answers has a more positive impact on your business?

A) "I am a dishwasher, but only until I can get a better job as an actor or a taxi driver. But I am thinking of going into politics."

B) "Well, I work in the kitchen of a local restaurant."

C) "Well, I work in the kitchen of a great local restaurant. Hey, here's my business card. Come to the restaurant and we will reward you with a complimentary appetizer. We love seeing familiar faces!"

If you answered "A" or "B", please consider starting this book over. "C" is the only correct answer.

(Now you know why a low cost investment in business cards, the back of which is a "Gift Certificate" for an appetizer or dessert, with restrictions, should become part of your marketing plan.)

Some of you, probably associated with upscale fine dining restaurants, may be shaking your head at this suggestion. "The customers I serve are probably not in the same social circles as my dishwashers, so having them hand out business cards is a waste."

Wrong. Your dishwasher may or may not generate fine dining customers for you, even with a certificate on the back of a business card. However, by giving him a business card, even without the "certificate" on the back, you increase the likelihood that he may find for you other employees, hopefully hardworking, who see the business card as an indication of the *respect* you provide all your employees. You win either way – new customers or new employees who seek you out.

You need to recruit and hire people who reflect positively on your restaurant, both inside and outside your four walls. The obvious methods for generating a list of candidates include: newspaper ads, Internet-based ads (frequently low or no-cost), a "help wanted" sign on your door, employee referrals, and soliciting your competitor's best employees.

Advertising for new employees is necessary, particularly if you are opening a new location, growing, or suffering from high turnover. Congratulations if your needs are primarily related to growth and expansion; however high turnover indicates a different problem. Either you are hiring incorrectly to begin with, you are hiring fine but training poorly, or hiring poorly and no amount of training will make a difference.

Employee referrals can be great, but be careful. A person tends to refer friends or associates who are somewhat similar to himself. Hard working, bright, energetic, and motivated people tend to hang out with similarly focused people. These recruits have a higher probability of success.

Your "bottom of the barrel" employees, and you know you have them too, may refer you a "winner", but you need to be more careful during your interview process to weed out those who may not properly align themselves with your corporate objectives.

Offer "Referral Bonuses" to your employees, but the bonuses are paid out only after a minimum amount of time has passed. For example, you may pay $100 to the referring employee when the new employee reaches four months with you, another $100 when the eight-month milestone is reached, and a final $100 on the one-year anniversary. After the third successful hire referred by an employee, throw in an extra $300. Higher rewards accompany longevity, and also contribute toward the continued employment of the original referring employee.

Hiring the incorrect employee is expensive in so many ways. The wrong person reduces the team's productivity. He turns off customers, mostly through an indifferent work ethic. He uses training resources that would have been better spent on the correct employee. Termination leads to a less desirable Worker's Unemployment Rating, resulting in a higher fee paid to the State Unemployment Commission across *all* your wages.

During an interview, every prospective employee will share his glorious successes in the foodservice industry. Obviously you should check references, but our highly litigious society makes the more honest evaluation, such as "he's okay but never let him near the cash register," extremely unlikely.

So what can you do? Actively find great restaurant employees by eating elsewhere, particularly in restaurants with a similar customer base as your own. You have the opportunity to evaluate a prospective employee's people skills in the most critical and informative ways possible: with you as a customer.

If you do not have the time to eat elsewhere due to the 70+ hour workweeks typically required of you (thanks to the inadequate people working for you), evaluate the skills of other people who service you during a typical week. Was the clerk at the local electronics store particularly helpful, and did he remind you to purchase batteries as well? Did the checkout person at your neighborhood store smile at you and engage in some conversation?

It is easier to train genuinely "nice" people already in a service-oriented position to represent your restaurant well, than it is to train someone to be nice (or at least fake it).

Use your web site to recruit new employees. Create a web page that speaks of your commitment to customers and employees. Include a link to your job application and ask candidates the following questions: 1) Why would you like to work at (restaurant name)? 2) What can you exceptionally contribute to (restaurant name)? 3) Describe your last experience while a customer at (restaurant name).

One final reminder about recruiting – it only ends for you the day you retire.

Interviewing and Testing

I recently witnessed the hiring of an employee at a restaurant that I personally enjoy very much. I happened to be at a meeting with the owner when someone walked in unexpectedly and inquired about a job.

The owner gave the candidate a form to fill out that included the usual requests for information. Five minutes later the interview started. "I see you worked here as a waiter, very good. What kind of restaurant was it? How busy did you get? When can you start?" Ten minutes later the interview was done.

The answers were clearly adequate because this candidate became a busboy that evening as I had my dinner in the restaurant.

This is not a criticism of the owner. As I said earlier, I enjoy this restaurant and both the food and service are truly exceptional. But I did wonder about how critical the interview process is for many restaurateurs, and if it needs to be improved.

The answer is a definite maybe. The skill requirements for some restaurant jobs require virtually no experience, just a desire to work. Other positions, such as Shift Managers and the critical General Manager position should not be filled in a ten-minute interview.

In speaking with restaurateurs, I learned that interviewing and testing candidates for communication skills and psychological traits ranges from minimal to extensive. The level of investment, both in time and hard dollars, correlates strongly with the type of restaurant, from

Independent to Franchise to Chain. (For you independent guys, this is another reason to find employees at competitive chains. They invest where you cannot, or have chosen not to. For my readers who are executives with chain restaurants, please ignore the last few sentences. If you are unable to do so, I commend you for your hiring practices – keep up the good work!)

I have some suggestions. All of your employees are important, but the level of investment in the hiring process should differ, depending on their compensation and level of importance to your success. You can continue taking some risks with your entry-level employees, but do not short-change the interview and reference check. If the employee has extensive contact with your customers, or manages numerous people, you need to be more systematic in your hiring process.

How can you get started? The best system for interviewing I have run across is called Topgrading. You can purchase the book, attend the seminar, or acquire an interactive training video from www.gazelles.com. This system leads to a superior percentage of correct hires. The higher the level in your organization, the more damaging an incorrect hire is to you, and the more rewarding the correct employee is to your organization.

In the service industry, some character traits are critical, many can be taught, and some need to be diligently avoided. Among the many books I have read, one book stands out as a classic and should be required reading for everyone in the service industry: "How to Win Friends and Influence People" by Dale Carnegie. Some of the examples may seem dated, but the principles are important and apply to your day-to-day customer interactions.

Training

Employees cannot perform the tasks you assign them if they are not properly trained, managed, and tested. And then trained some more.

Let us start with an example from outside the restaurant industry, a retail chain, privately held, that started as an independent.

In the retail industry the average length of training is 7 hours. This particular retailer provides 235 hours of training in the first year for its full time employees, and 160 hours of training for its part time workers. As a consumer, given the option, where would you shop if you needed assistance regarding a particular product?

The average employee turnover in this industry is over 100%, while this particular retailer typically has 15% to 25% turnover. Whose employees do you think are more productive?

This retailer needs fewer employees to generate more sales, and pays its employees more than the competition. They are proof of the adage that you are better off with a single motivated, well-trained, conscientious $16 per hour employee than two average performers earning an hourly wage of $8.

This retailer, The Container Store, only hires employees who care about excellence and are passionate about their jobs. Many of their employees are customers who were recruited by store employees. The Container

Store seems to always be in the top 10 of the annual "Fortune's Best Companies to Work For" list.

I hope you have not dismissed this as not being applicable to you, because it is. Even if you only operate a single restaurant, finding the right people, training them extensively, motivating them through better benefits and higher compensation (which could be based on profit, it does not have to be in their base salary) are all critical to increased success.

If you are an executive from a restaurant chain, you may be further along in this area than your colleagues who are independents. But do not be so sure; for every chain restaurant where I have received commendable service from obviously well trained employees, I have experienced pitiful service at another chain restaurant.

Necessary Server Traits

Some people are naturally friendlier than others. You may be one of those people, but if not, you certainly know them. They seem to always have a genuinely warm smile, easily converse with everyone, and wish you a "nice day" when you leave, again with a smile. Hire these people for every position that interacts with customers. (It helps to marry this type of person as well!) If you cannot find a truly friendly person, do not settle for the naturally "surly" type, or even for someone who can fake the "friendly" attribute. Their true self tends to reveal itself at inopportune moments, like when the most important restaurant reviewer in town is at your restaurant.

Good servers are knowledgeable about your food offerings across the entire menu. They can tell you how dishes are prepared, and what entrees are enhanced with specific wines. If you have a food allergy or just dislike a particular ingredient, they can be helpful even if they need to verify the answer with a chef, without appearing clueless. They can describe today's specials fluently without mispronouncing the name of the entrée.

Have you ever repeatedly looked around for your server, or any restaurant employee, to ask a question or get assistance with a problem? Good servers will be aware of customer needs throughout their shifts. Good restaurants will train all their wait staff to be aware of customer needs and support each other on the floor.

Servers need to be available to customers. It is still possible to be accessible even when serving multiple tables or retrieving food items from the kitchen. The lack of this trait is observed when servers waste time with "mini-breaks" or have friendly conversations with co-workers away from their customers.

Communicating with customers, including small talk, describing menu items, and gently selling coffee and desserts is such an obvious requirement, but when not prioritized, costs you severely. Servers who inadequately describe menu items cause you to lose revenue. Establishing a minimal rapport with customers is necessary to make diners feel that they are in a warm and sociable environment. The act of merely offering desserts to diners at the end of a fine meal, or chips and queso to the customer buying a burrito, will ultimately provide significant increased profits to you.

You do need to be cautious about servers who are "overly friendly" and interrupt your customers' conversations. There is a balance between great service and intrusive behavior.

Teach your employees to be proactive by anticipating and delivering before requests are even made. You typically refill soda, iced tea and coffee when requested, so do not wait to be asked. Keep those cups and glasses filled. I can remember too many meals where my diet soda was empty and I was left sucking on ice cubes until my server finally came around. Always pleasant about returning with a refill after I asked, their inability to proactively anticipate my needs was a failure. You can say it even motivated me to "proactively" find another restaurant.

It goes without saying that servers need to be clean and groomed, even in a biker bar. (Tattoos that may be inappropriate at your favorite fondue restaurant are, however, a bonus in this other restaurant category.) Uniforms should not be stained, food or otherwise. I once waited in line at a Mexican quick service restaurant. When I approached the counter to place my order I noticed that the order-taker/cashier had dirt caked under his fingernails. My mind quickly raced through the probabilities that the workers preparing my food would have just come from the same playground. I opted for safety; I ordered a small soda and went elsewhere for lunch. This was over two years ago and I have not returned to that restaurant. Fortunately, I found two other fast casual Mexican restaurants near my office to replace this one. The food is more costly, but not nearly as psychologically expensive as the alternative.

Finally, enable your servers to be problem solvers. Issues arise; food is prepared incorrectly, not delivered as timely as it should have been, or just is not pleasing to the customer's palate. Let the server offer complimentary dessert or coffee without having to speak with you first. You can worry about blame or justification later; right now it is time to turn a negative experience into a positive one. You will not be able to accomplish this unless your servers are trusted and allowed to use their own good judgment. You should try to greet these inconvenienced diners as well before they leave. Now that your server has neutralized the negative (hopefully), your personal arrival is desirable to encourage a return visit in the near future so your restaurant can "provide the level of service" you take pride in. Although "perfection" is next to impossible, "near-perfection" is obtainable for you.

➤ What can you do to ensure quality "recruits" are always being pursued?

➤ How can you improve your interviewing skills so you can avoid the losers and increase the probability of hiring gems?

➤ What can you do to improve your training program so that your employees are motivated, effective, and aligned with your goals?

➤ The best servers in the industry share these traits: they are friendly, knowledgeable, available, good communicators, proactive, clean, and problem solvers.

"The age of your children is a key factor in how quickly you are served in a restaurant. We once had a waiter in Canada who said, 'Could I get you your check?' and we answered, "How about the menu first?"'

Erma Bombeck

Chapter 8

'T' ?
TOP-OF-MIND
IS PRIME REAL ESTATE

February 3, 8:13 AM

*T*he drive to work typically takes Eric about 15 minutes, but this morning he was running some errands first and didn't even plan on being in the restaurant until about 10:00 AM.

Following his "lessons" with Dana regarding the first two principles in ENTRÉE Marketing^{SM}, creating a restaurant that "entices" people back, and the need for employees to provide "near-perfect service", he realized these were areas in which he could dramatically improve.

He started by creating a list of capital improvements, such as lighting, a better sound system, some framed posters or original art, new bathroom fixtures, and a medium-sized plasma screen TV for the waiting area.

The estimated cost of these items was added, along with a time line for implementation and a weighing of the proposed cost versus the benefit. Surprisingly, it looked like his investment would not be as high as he had initially feared.

Finding reliable vendors to install electrical and plumbing items, assist in designing and printing new menus, and provide server training for his new "service-oriented" employees posed a different challenge.

Dana once again provided him with the solution. "Aren't you a member of your restaurant association? They have a category of Allied Members who provide products and services to the restaurant members. You know they are familiar with your industry and their success is dependent on your success."

Eric was not a member but he did recall that an association had called him prior to his opening up the restaurant. He may even have received some mail from them as recently as a few months ago regarding some legislative issues that would hurt the restaurant industry. Although he had met with a representative – wasn't his name Joe? - he had dismissed the idea of joining at the time because he was focused on other things, and "it wasn't in the budget."

A quick search on the Internet identified the Restaurant Association of Maryland (RAM). His email inquiry to the association generated a return call that same day. It was Joe again, and he remembered Eric from their meeting almost two years ago.

They spoke briefly and Eric explained that he was looking for trusted vendors to help with some restaurant issues. The call concluded with an invitation from Joe to attend the next RAM-Frederick County Chapter Meeting with other restaurateurs and a promise to send a list of potential vendors. Before the end of the day, Eric had an email and a fax from Joe with exactly the information he needed.

Eric turned into a local lighting store and picked up the fixtures he had ordered a few days before. He carefully placed the lighting fixtures in his vehicle and within minutes was on the highway heading for the Circuit City electronics store to purchase the plasma TV. He had received a timely email with a coupon for 10% off, and even though it was a little further away than other electronics stores, he felt the savings was worth the extra time.

It was still early and Eric, who had stopped only for a cup of coffee at a conveniently located Dunkin Donuts, was feeling hungry.

While considering various options for a quick breakfast, a billboard came into view. "Arby's new breakfast menu" was the subject and that helped Eric make up his mind. He took the next exit and within minutes was biting into a tasty Sourdough Egg and Cheese sandwich. Another pretty good cup of coffee was on the table in front of him. "I didn't even know they served breakfast," he thought.

What is "Top-of-Mind"?

Top-of-mind: *adj*. First thing somebody thinks about, what is present in the uppermost level of consciousness.

Look around your restaurant and observe your customers. You have so many different people coming through the door. You might spot them while they are waiting to be seated, or as they are enjoying their food. They may be dining by themselves, with a few friends, part of a large group, or just grabbing something quickly to take back to their office or home. It may be a family enjoying a meal out together, possibly celebrating a special occasion. Despite the differences they all share one thing in common.

For this day, for one meal, *your restaurant was "top-of-mind" to them.*

It may have been accidental; they could be with someone else who chose the restaurant. You may have been an alternative choice; their first choice may have had a long line or no reservations available at a convenient time for them.

Whatever factor made you their choice is irrelevant for the moment because once they are dining with you, your ability to meet, or even better, surpass their expectations for this meal becomes critical to your being top-of-mind with them tomorrow.

The first two principles we learned about, "Enticing" and "Near-Perfect Service" provide you the understanding and guidelines for adjusting your four-walls marketing to position yourself as a "top-of-mind" restaurant to your customers.

The primary purpose of all your marketing and advertising is to obtain for you this coveted position in your customers' minds. Loyal customers certainly think of you first when choosing a restaurant in your category, but you can even influence a non-customer with the right advertising at the right time.

It starts by understanding advertising strategies, as well as the advantages and disadvantages of various media options. We will examine some common advertising strategies in this chapter, and take a more thorough look at various media options in Chapter 12.

Reach and Frequency

"Reach" is part of every promotional effort you implement on behalf of your restaurant, including permission-based email, community events, local or big city newspapers, and mass media.

It is defined simply as the number of people that are "exposed" to your message. With print media your theoretical reach starts with the gross circulation number. Yellow Pages advertising touts the number of directories distributed in a given market; that is the reach they provide. Prime time TV may give you a reach in the millions.

As illustrated above, the advertising vehicle you choose determines your reach. Choose incorrectly and you waste your money, as the people who are exposed to your ad are not prospective customers for you anyway. Choose correctly and you have the chance to generate business from new customers and repeat visits from occasional customers.

"Frequency" is the number of times that the same target market is exposed to your advertising. Since advertising has been demonstrated to have a cumulative effect, the more frequently your prospect is exposed to your message, the more likely she will consider dining at your restaurant.

When creating your restaurant's marketing objectives and deciding on strategy, reach and frequency work together to consume your time and budget. "Everything in life is a tradeoff" could easily have been coined by an advertising sales representative trying to get you to change your media plan and buy his product.

In regard to competing with other chain restaurants that have a significant marketing budget, this is an area where the independent is at a significant disadvantage. The independent restaurateur can create as good, or an even better menu, and she can provide the same high level, or an even higher, more personalized level of service than the chain location down the street. Check out Da Mimmo in Baltimore's Little Italy area and you will experience the "independent's edge." But with a relatively limited budget, the independent will never be able to outspend the chain in reach and frequency.

Fortunately, better decisions lead to better results, even with a smaller budget. A common mistake made by restaurateurs is to trade greater reach for less frequency. For example, an independent pizzeria has the opportunity to reach 20,000 households within 20 miles of its location, or 5,000 households within 5 miles. The per-mailer price at quantity 20,000 is 18% less expensive than the per mailer price for quantity 5,000. The sales representative for the coupon company recommends the greater "reach", 20,000 homes, and also suggests extending the deadline to redeem the coupon an extra month.

His explanation: "We will create a great coupon for you and you'll be flooded with business. You know, some of our customers have seen redemption rates as high as 6%! Can you imagine that? You could have 1,200 new customers in your restaurant just this month! And when it works, you'll reinvest a portion of your profit back into this program and we will do it again."

His fear: if you plan to send to fewer homes multiple times and you are disappointed after two mailings, you will not continue the program. In his mind, he is better off getting your money and his full commission immediately because there are too many reasons you may not continue.

Please do not consider this a knock against sales people from coupon mailing companies. Bad sales reps like this exist in every industry. Your radio rep will try to sell you as much as she can, as will your cable TV rep, newspaper rep, magazine rep, etc.

It is your responsibility to know what you need to do to grow your restaurant, just as it is the sale representatives' responsibility to generate revenue for his company.

By the way, the sales person's fears are not unjustified. Too often the inexperienced restaurateur bails on advertising because the results are not good. The disappointing results are usually the result of an action plan that was lousy to begin with. Minimal advertising, done randomly, at the wrong time, aimed at too large a market, and in response to declining business is a wonderful recipe for failure.

Declining business usually generates one of three actions:

1) "Business is down; we'd better cut back on our marketing because we have less revenue!" This usually indicates that restaurant supplies, fixtures and equipment will soon be available for a bargain price because the owner will be selling mortgage refinancing in his brother-in-law's company in the near future.

2) "Business is down; we'd better run some ads immediately!" This response is not uncommon from restaurateurs who have focused on everything but marketing, but understand its importance.

3) "Business is down; let's figure out why and see if we have to modify our marketing plan based on what we learn. Also, let's go over the response rates from our various media at this week's marketing meeting. By the way, did you catch the ending of that football game yesterday?"

Recency Theory

I first heard Erwin Ephron speak at an Outdoor Advertising Conference. Mr. Ephron is acknowledged as the "Father of Recency Planning" and his work has influenced the world of media planning like few others.

His Recency Theory caused shock waves and concern in an industry that takes satisfaction in being ahead of the curve, or actually prides itself on creating the curve.

The Recency Theory states that although advertising provides knowledge and awareness of a product, it is wasted on all consumers, except those who are in the market for that product. The reason for this is simple. If you are not paying attention to the ad, it is useless. And you only pay attention to an ad when it addresses a product need that you have. Advertising itself does not create awareness; rather it is your brain, rapidly filtering the 3,000+ ads it is exposed to every day, and finding 6 that are of value to you at that point in your life.

Simple example: A reasonable quantity of the ads and images you are exposed to every day is for automobiles. If you are not in the market for a new car, these ads are wasted on you. Sooner or later, you will be in the market for a new car and your brain will start opening itself up to these ads as you begin gathering information about available options suitable with your needs. As you narrow down your choices, car ads for vehicles that do not meet your requirements will again be filtered out. Eventually you will purchase a car and no car ads will penetrate your brain until the process starts all over again. (One exception: you will notice ads for the vehicle you acquired for some time after the purchase. It is a way of reassuring you that you made a good decision.)

How does this relate to your advertising? Fortunately most people eat out multiple times a week so they are always choosing a restaurant. Your ad will not be blocked out because it does not meet a need, but it can be quickly disregarded for other reasons. If your restaurant is not a "destination restaurant" and faces numerous competitors in the same niche, you can be eliminated purely based on distance. Most people will choose from multiple pizzerias within three miles from their home or office rather than travel six miles simply because they were exposed to your ad.

In regard to Recency, the timing of your ad is more important. If you are exposed to a billboard ad while you are hungry, that ad has a powerful message for you. If you drive by that same billboard ad after having just eaten, it's meaningless.

> ➤ Choose greater frequency over more reach to maximize sales and minimize wasted ad dollars.
> ➤ Some media options can be timed to maximize interest in your ads. If you are promoting special weekend events your ads should be timed to reach the consumer during the middle of the week.
> ➤ All of your marketing efforts have the ultimate goal of making you top-of-mind to as many of your customers as possible.
> ➤ You can increase the percentage of your customers who afford you top-of-mind status. You need to start by identifying them and targeting them with extra marketing efforts. Loyalty, frequent dining programs, and permission-based communications like email and direct mail, are very effective.
> ➤ Advertising has the greatest impact when consumers are ready to buy.

"I know half my marketing is wasted. Trouble is, I don't know which half!"

Viscount Leverhulme, Founder of Unilever

Chapter 9

'R' ?
REWARDS ARE AN
ESSENTIAL MOTIVATOR

February 9, 10:12 PM

*T*he day was coming to an end; just one more detail left to ensure her upcoming business trip wasn't only business. The convenience of the Internet would allow her to make a dinner reservation in Las Vegas, 2700 miles away, without having to personally call anyone and risk being put on hold.*

It had been a long day. Dana had an early morning meeting and she had stopped at a bagel store to pick up bagels for the office. "Only one more visit and I have a dozen free bagels coming," she thought when the clerk handed her back her change and Bagel Club card.

After the meeting with her co-workers, she began making her reservations for the upcoming trip. She logged on to the web sites from two airlines to compare prices and schedules. They were pretty similar, so she made her online economy reservation with the airline that gave her an extra thousand

*points for booking online. She then upgraded her
ticket to First Class using miles she had earned.*

*Next she took care of her hotel and rental car.
She was accumulating points in different hotel loyalty
clubs, but she chose the hotel that had just sent her
an email with special rates and amenities that
coincided with the dates of her trip. Her rental choice
rarely changed. The company she virtually always
used provided her with an automatic upgrade to a
full-size car when she booked a medium-sized car
because of her membership in their club.*

*She paid for the airline ticket with her American
Express card and earned points for gifts or travel.
She used her MasterCard for the hotel reservation
because there was a joint promotion between the
hotel and credit card that provided "double points".
She used her Visa for the rental car and again earned
points for future redemption. She made sure as well
that points would be properly awarded between the
hotel, airline and rental car company, as the
programs were tied into each other.*

*Lunchtime led her to Burrito Beach for soup and
salad, and Dana earned double points with the email
she had printed. She was alternating her lunchtime
activities between eating, working out at the gym,
and occasionally shopping. The gym had just
introduced a new referral program and she was
reminded to invite some friends who had commented
about joining a gym. On her quick shopping trip to
Nordstrom's (she loved how service oriented they
were!), the clerk mentioned that she had just earned
a $50 gift certificate and it would be sent to her soon.*

She left work just after 6:00 PM and stopped to return a DVD at the video rental store. There was no charge because she had earned a coupon for a free rental. Adjacent to the video place was a bookstore and she purchased the latest book by Dr. Phil. This was discounted because she belonged to their Book Club.

She had two more stops before finally getting home. First was the gas station, where she paid with their branded card and saved 6 cents per gallon. Then she stopped at the grocery store to pick up enough items to get her through the weekend. The receipt she was provided by the cashier noted that she had saved $6.24 using her grocery card.

Her day was drawing to a close. All that remained were dinner reservations at two restaurants she enjoyed. Both of these restaurants made the effort to invite her back, Commander's Palace and Gaetano's with their email programs. This was completed in moments, and now she was ready to watch one of her digitally recorded TV shows, without the commercials of course.

Motivating by Rewarding

re-ward:

n. Something given or received in payment for worthy behavior.

v. 1) To bestow a reward on.

2) To give a reward because of or in return for.

There are multiple motivators of human behavior; two of the most common are compensation of value to the recipient and fear of a negative result. "The carrot or the stick" is a popular expression used to concisely describe these approaches.

The "fear" approach is rarely seen in consumer advertising, except for political campaigns. Motivating a choice "away" from a competing product (or person) can be very risky to the advertiser.

Can you imagine a restaurant advertisement soliciting business like this? "Dine in elegance at Sweet Meadow restaurant. We have considerably fewer health code violations than our competition!"

Maybe it works for you, but I would stay home and rent a movie.

What works best is a reward of value to the consumer. Think of it however you wish: payment, incentive, gift, compensation, coupon, certificate, diner-loyalty program, or bribery. Reward programs unquestionably work, the challenges include finding appropriate rewards for your customers that are relevant, have a high perceived value, are easy for your staff to understand, and are not too costly to implement and maintain.

Too often we tend to think of an obvious restaurant reward: free food. This can be appropriate at times, but does not necessarily accomplish your marketing objectives. For example, promoting a "Buy One Get One Free" too frequently can train your customers to only eat at your restaurant when this offer is available, ignoring you and eating elsewhere all other times.

The rewards you provide are limited only by your creativity. Over twenty-five years ago American Airlines introduced the first frequent flyer program, eternally changing our perception of "customer loyalty." There had been formal and informal loyalty and rewards programs prior to the AAdvantage program, such as the bartender pouring a free drink to a favored customer, but the ambitious program launched by American Airlines became a case study and model for many industries.

Through partnerships you can now use your American Airlines miles (points) to travel around the world, even on other airlines that have reciprocal arrangements with American. You can even earn enough miles for a free airline ticket without ever flying American, just by using an affiliated credit card. You can earn additional miles by using the credit card and eating in a restaurant affiliated with their program.

What about rewards? The obvious ones are free trips and seat upgrades. Equally valuable for many business travelers are priority-boarding, access to private airport clubs between flights, and economy plus seating with 5 inches of extra legroom. Hotels, rental cars, retail products and even Internet services are now linked to the program. AAdvantage has evolved significantly since its introduction, and continues to change in response to competitive programs and consumer preferences.

It is hard to find an industry today that does not have some type of reward program in place. (Okay – the medical industry is a major exception. But the appeal of a

"Buy eight surgeries of your choice and the ninth one is on us!" may be limited.)

Restaurant Rewards

Most restaurants that have some type of reward or incentive program in place to maintain top-of-mind status with its customers and encourage more frequent visits, uses one or more of the following approaches.

The first reward type is primarily "emotional." Your customer is psychologically rewarded for dining with you. This can include a gracious "hello" and addressing the customer by name. Some restaurants go further and create a "Wall of Fame" that has photographs or caricatures of frequent diners. Aside from generating repeat visits, these honored diners bring their friends, thereby creating larger tickets for you.

Coupons and certificates are unquestionably "rewards." For those of you who would never think of providing a "coupon," do not be so quick to eliminate this very valuable promotional method. Coupons work because the customer: 1) pays attention to your restaurant ad, 2) obtains value in the form of a discount that may not be currently available with your competition, and 3) is immediately rewarded for choosing your restaurant.

Coupons are also an effective way to track the value of the offer. Redeemed coupons are associated with the sales volume they bring in, and over time may be integrated into your pricing. I have lunch at least once a week at a pizza and sub shop near my office. For as long as I can remember, every time I purchased my meal there was a coupon on the tray offering "75 cents off an 8" sub." I always have this coupon when I visit the restaurant. I do not know the percentage of these redemptions, but as the coupon is always available, it seems reasonable that the discount is already built into the price. On the occasional day when I forget the coupon, they have provided me the "discounted" price anyway.

Okay – you are not a pizza and sub shop and cannot imagine providing a "coupon" in your full service fine dining establishment. Fine – provide a "gift certificate."

What is the primary difference between a coupon and a gift certificate? Answer: the price of the entrée.

Does this work for fine dining restaurants? Will a "coupon on steroids," a "fancy gift certificate," make a difference to fine dining restaurant patrons? To some of us, absolutely! As I am writing this I have a "Gift Certificate" from The Palm offering me $25 off when I purchase two entrees. There is some fine print, but nothing unusual. I will use the Gift Certificate, and because I will likely go with family or friends, we will probably still spend $150 - $200 on this dinner. What is the cost to The Palm for this promotion? They will "lose" $25 in revenue off the total bill (which they may not have received without the certificate). This equates to $7 - $10 in food costs, depending on what we order.

Calling it a coupon or a certificate makes no difference as long as you understand that this incentive brings customers through your doors.

A cousin of this low cost "reward" program is the card that is stamped or marked to indicate a purchase.

Following a defined quantity of purchases (total dollars spent is irrelevant), the consumer receives something free. Subway implemented an effective program that provided a free sandwich after 10 sandwiches had been purchased. (This program did run into problems with fraud in various markets and had to be modified.)

There is a significant psychological difference between a coupon/certificate reward versus a "buy 7 and get the 8th free" reward. We all have a balance between our desires for immediate gratification versus a long-term payout. Some people opt for a job right out of high school to begin earning an immediate income. Other people choose, if the opportunity exists, to extend their education and be rewarded potentially with different skills and higher income years later.

Coupons and certificates provide immediate gratification. No additional cards to continue carrying around in your purse or wallet are necessary. You make your purchase decision and you are immediately rewarded with a percentage discount, a few dollars off, or complimentary chips and guacamole.

However, the restaurant card requiring only three more visits to earn a free sandwich assists in keeping that restaurant top-of-mind. This assumes of course, that the consumer can live with his wallet or her purse getting fatter as more and more cards from different vendors are received.

What about more high-end reward program options? In this category we include point-based programs that provide a reward after the customer has accumulated sufficient points over time. Customer spending is the driver in this type of program, and that requires an accounting and tracking system to ensure the customer is properly rewarded. Regular communication with your customers is a must to ensure the points remain a motivator.

A point-based program is more expensive and complicated, and most restaurants will hire an outside company to manage the technological details. But technology is easing the entry into a point-based program for many restaurants.

A significant advantage of the points-based program is the larger variety of rewards you can offer, thereby enabling you to attract more customers to the program. Since your customers are motivated by different incentives, a variety of rewards and levels have the best potential for contributing to more frequent returns.

One restaurant program I have enrolled in provides a combination of Gift Certificates that are sent to me via email or direct mail, and a point-based program that keeps track of my spending. The Gift Certificate provides an immediate payoff and my visit still contributes toward the bigger awards that are achieved over time.

I can trade my points for many types of rewards, including rewards that are only marginally related, or even completely unrelated to the restaurant. Gift Certificates for the restaurant range from $35 to $120, or I can order an autographed cookbook. Other rewards include Gift Certificates at high-end retailers like Tiffany & Company and Neiman Marcus, as well as vacation packages, including a trip to any of their restaurants throughout the country.

The key areas for you to focus on when creating a rewards program include:

1) Rewards have to have legitimate value to the customer, and if points-based, should offer a variety of awards to account for different customer preferences. This type of program will require an investment in technology to track accumulated points and provide frequent communication with your customers.

2) The program should be clear and understandable to your customers. Lack of clarity leads to confusion and disappointment.

3) Your staff needs to understand and implement the program, so clarity for them is equally critical. As you may expect them to participate in signing-up your customers for the program, they should be trained on how to "sell" the program, and have a good understanding of the benefits your customers can obtain.

4) Management of the program includes monitoring your competition and adding new prize levels and bonuses on occasion. The program American Airlines offers its AAdvantage members is very different than the program that was originally introduced.

Remember – rewarding people to motivate desired behavior is as old as mankind. It can take many forms, and the reward can be as simple as truly the finest food and service in your city. That may be sufficient, as the ability to get a table at your unique and remarkable restaurant is reward enough for many customers. For the rest of us mortals, a little extra "something" is equally important.

> ➢ As a consumer, what recognition, extra benefits, or rewards would motivate you to eat at a local restaurant more frequently? Will these same rewards work for your customers?
> ➢ What tangible rewards would motivate your customers to invite their friends to join them for a meal at your restaurant?
> ➢ How can a reward program be used to increase "word-of-mouth" referrals for your restaurant?
> ➢ Can you provide the attention needed to make a more complicated "point-based program successful, or should you start with a simpler coupon/certificate program?

"My mother's menu consisted of two choices: Take it or leave it."

Buddy Hackett

Chapter **10**

'E' ?
THE EIGHTY-TWENTY RULE
CAN MAKE LIFE SIMPLER

February 23, 3:05 PM

*L**unch was busier than usual and there was a sense of growing accomplishment among the workforce at Fish Outta Water. Well - most of the workforce. There were still a handful of employees who seemed less motivated and reluctant to change their behaviors, as evidenced by their frequent tardiness and the extra management attention they needed.*

"Fortunately, it's only a minority of my employees, but they sure cause me the most headaches," thought Eric to himself as he prepared for a meeting with Dana.

It had been just over a month since he began working with her, and Eric was grateful that he had attended Dana's marketing presentation at his local bank. Using the four principles he had already learned, numerous changes had been made within the restaurant.

Some of the changes required physical improvements to make the restaurant more enticing to customers. A plasma TV had been added in the bar area, fixtures were upgraded in the restrooms, lighting was improved throughout the restaurant, and more seating was to be added in the waiting area. These improvements required some capital investment, and even though cash was tight, Eric saw the wisdom in enhancing the restaurant's atmosphere.

Other changes were ongoing, starting with a more extensive training program for all employees who interacted with customers. Familiarity with menu items, learning about wines and feeling confident in making recommendations, increased sensitivity to customer needs, and gently "selling" desserts to finish a great meal were the first areas of training introduced. If "perfect" service wasn't possible, striving for it still was!

A new marketing plan was being written and all of the elements were geared toward establishing Fish Outta Water as the "top-of-mind" restaurant for a greater percentage of the restaurant's customers. A larger share of the total marketing budget was being allocated to "four walls" marketing, with the remainder of the budget used to target all existing customers, as well as potential customers within five miles of the restaurant, mostly through community events and networking.

A formal diner loyalty and rewards program was also being developed. Eric wanted to move very quickly in this area, but Dana was urging him to speak with customers first and see what it was that they felt would be valuable to them. "It doesn't make sense to introduce ten reward levels," she said, "when only two or three of them are important to your customers." Eric compromised, while working on the details of the program, he made sure to spend more time meeting customers and even "buying" some of them dessert in appreciation for their patronage.

A lot of progress had been made in just one month. Eric was pleased with the restaurant's advancement, but he was still very tired. His long work hours and attention to every detail were keeping him away from home and his family. "When I am finished implementing the ENTRÉE Marketing^{SM} program, I need to schedule a family vacation," he thought to himself. "Let's see, where should we go?"

His vacation planning was interrupted, however as Dana entered his office. "Have you ever heard of Vilfredo Pareto?" she asked.

"Is he a travel agent? I desperately need help planning a vacation."

"No," responded Dana. "He is much more important. If you figure out how to use what he learned, you will have time for that vacation, and more."

Pareto's Principle / The 80 – 20 Rule

Pa-re-to, Vilfredo. 1848 – 1923. Italian economist.

Parerto's Principle: A small number of causes (20%) are responsible for a large percentage (80%) of the effect.

You may have heard the expression "20% of your customers account for 80% of your revenue." It is based on an expansion of research first done by Mr. Pareto in England during the early 1900's.

Mr. Pareto's research indicated that 20% of the people in England owned 80% of the wealth. This finding was very intriguing and his research was expanded. He then studied similar data going back a full century and discovered that roughly these same percentages were accurate. A wealthy elite, although relatively small as a percentage of the population, controlled the majority of wealth. Further motivated, he extended his research to other European countries, and the findings remained consistent. Despite different cultures, political systems, levels of industrialization and personal freedoms, the 80/20 Rule was consistent.

A small minority owned a disproportionate share of resources. We were soon to learn, through the research of Dr. Joseph Juran in the 1930's and 1940's that this principle applied to far more than just the distribution of wealth.

Dr. Juran was an expert in Quality Management. In his studies he found that 80% of a product's defects could be traced back to problems in 20% of the manufacturing line. This led to his rule regarding the "vital few and trivial many." In regard to quality control, 20% of "something" is responsible for 80% of the outcome.

The percentages do not have to exactly equal 20 and 80, nor does the sum have to total 100. The concept, without the numbers, is critical. A small percentage of something has a disproportionately large impact.

Okay – so we know this applies to wealth distribution, including income, and manufacturing. Does it apply as well to real life, and most importantly, to restaurant management?

Two books by Richard Koch, *The 80/20 Principle* and *The 80/20 Individual* are excellent guides to identifying and using the 80/20 Rule in everyday life and work.

Let us start with our homes. You can carpet your entire home the day you move in. Certain high traffic areas in your home will require more maintenance and replacement than the rest of the carpeted areas. In my home, the carpet between the garage and the stairs leading up to the main level has been replaced three times, no other carpet in the house has needed replacement. Accumulated dirt in other high traffic areas requires cleaning on a more frequent basis.

What about outside the home? A minority of drivers causes the great majority of traffic accidents. These "accident-prone" drivers are typically younger (relatively new and inexperienced), or from the "Greatest Generation" (elderly with slowing reflexes), or problem drinkers, or habitual traffic law violators.

The rule is important in business. When introducing a new product, marketing needs to be geared towards the "vital few" who are early adopters by nature, and likely to share their experiences with their friends. Advertising efforts that attempt to encompass the entire potential market are wasted as the "trivial many" ignore your product until it has mass acceptance.

Applying Pareto's Principle to Restaurants

Now we will examine how the 80/20 Principle applies to the restaurant industry.

During a business trip to Chicago, I had dinner at The Cheesecake Factory restaurant near my hotel. Following dinner, the server returned the menu so I could consider dessert. I counted the number of desserts, the bulk of which were, not surprisingly, different cheesecakes. The total quantity approached 40. I asked the server which desserts were most popular. She immediately identified about 5, and when I did not jump at those suggestions, she added a few more. Out of 40 desserts, her customers ordered 7 to 10 different options most frequently. Granted, this was not a scientific study, and I do not have access to food sales by menu items from The Cheesecake Factory. But I would be very surprised if a few of their dessert items did not account for a disproportionately large volume of dessert sales. (By the way, I did not order any of the top choices. I selected the low-carb cheesecake.)

Within your restaurant you can apply Pareto's Principle to your operations, employees, marketing, sales, and your profits.

Operations and Employees

Operationally, 20% of your suppliers provide 80% of your stock, and 20% of your inventory takes up 80% of the space. Are you too dependent on some suppliers? In the event of a shortage, do you have alternative suppliers that can fill your needs? As a loyal customer to some of your suppliers, are you being properly rewarded with exceptional service and discounts?

Your employees fit Pareto's Principle, both positively and negatively. A small percentage of your employees are very replaceable, not because the job itself requires minimal skills, but rather their work ethic leaves much to be desired. These are the employees who are late most frequently, and call in with the most undocumented "sick" days. This 20% probably generates 80% of your customer complaints.

The flip side of this coin is the group of employees on the other end of the spectrum. These are the employees you would love to clone. They represent you well to your customers. They support your brand, rather than detract from it. They generated frequent compliments, and the highest average tips. This "vital few" 20% generates 80% of your add-on sales, extra appetizers, salads, drinks, coffee and desserts.

Marketing and Media Choices

Although marketing is critical, some marketing efforts are more vital to your success than others, and some efforts have a relatively minimal impact.

If you could only choose three (or even four) of these options to increase the likelihood of your success this year, which options would you choose?

- TV – Network or Cable
- Radio
- Newspaper
- Magazine / Directory (Dining Guide)
- Yellow Pages
- Coupon Mailers
- Direct Mail to Customer List
- Permission-based Email
- "Four-walls" marketing and promotions
- Community sponsorships
- Billboards / Outdoor Media
- Web site
- Word of mouth
- Internet: Banner Ads and Search Engines
- Public Relations

Applying Pareto's Principle to your choices can save you money and increase your revenue. If you are spending 80% of your budget and only obtaining 20% of the results, you need to modify your formula. Some of these options are a fraction of the cost of other options, yet they will bring you superior and measurable results.

It costs considerably more to attract a new customer into your restaurant than it does to get an existing occasional customer to increase his frequency. Your marketing plan needs to address the need for both new customers and greater loyalty from existing customers. Pareto's Law can help you better prioritize the resources you use to achieve these goals.

Revenue and Profitability

Many restaurateurs I work with recognize the disproportionate revenue contributions provided by their best customers. If as Pareto's Law would suggest, 20% of your customers are providing 80% of your revenue, we have an opportunity to grow your revenue considerably. What are the characteristics of these critical "best" customers? How frequently do they visit? What are their favorite foods, and their average tickets? What restaurant traits appeal to them?

With this knowledge we can focus our attention on your occasional customers. Provide the same or equally important "emotional" rewards to these customers with the confidence that even one extra meal per month per customer can become a large increase in gross annual revenue. Your revenue grows and your percentages may change; instead of 20/80 you may find that 25% of your customers (those who think of you first, eat with you most frequently, and bring in the most new customers) may still account for 80% of your revenue.

Are some of your food items more profitable than others? It is likely that a smaller proportion of your total food offerings provide a disproportionate percentage of your profits. For example, a large pizza may sell for $16, as may a veal francese entree. Despite the equivalent sales price, the cost of food is lower for the pizza, resulting in a higher gross margin and profit for that menu item. If you have too many lower margin menu items competing at the same price as higher margin items, you may want to consider altering some prices.

What other revenue and profit analysis could you consider? What small percentage of your menu items account for your greatest sales and profitability? What food items cause you more losses due to spoilage? What infrequently used foods require a larger percentage of your refrigeration or freezer space? Beyond what distance in travel are the catering jobs reducing your margins?

Equally important, particularly for those restaurateurs who never have enough time regardless of the hours they work, is this application of Pareto's Law. In allocating your time, in understanding your impact on your restaurant's success, 20% of your decisions produce 80% of the results. So when you figure out which decisions are important for you to make, and delegate the others to your most capable employees (the top 20% of course!), your business will actually improve, and you will be able to reduce your working hours.

One final thought – no matter how great you become, 80% of your complaints will come from 20% of your customers. Some of these complaints will have merit and by responding to them, you and your staff will provide a better meal and atmosphere to all your clients. Of course, some of the complaints need to be ignored, especially if they request you to change your brand image to meet their needs. Remember, if you try to be all things to every one of your customers, you inevitably end up satisfying no one.

> ➤ There is a formula commonly known as the 80/20 Rule that was first recognized a century ago and impacts your restaurant today.
>
> ➤ Pareto's Law has very a very powerful application to your restaurant, including operations, employees, menu decisions, marketing, revenue and profitability.
>
> ➤ Properly applied, this principle affects your decisions related to vendors, employee training and retention, and media selection. It can save you money and increase your revenue.
>
> ➤ No one can "buy" more time, but we can use our time more efficiently. Pareto's Law helps us understand that as owners and managers different decisions impact the success of our business considerably. We need to focus on the 20% of issues that are critical to our success, and let others take the lead in making decisions on the less critical 80% of the issues that need attention.

"Only Irish Coffee provides in a single glass all four essential food groups: alcohol, caffeine, sugar and fat."
Alex Levine

Chapter 11

'E' ?
EMAIL MARKETING IS A
NECESSARY FOUNDATION

March 12, 6:24 PM

*F*ish Outta Water was breaking new ground today. It had started at lunchtime, as servers began collecting information from diners to use in a loyalty and reward program.

As the check was presented, each server added a few extra sentences to their standard expression of appreciation. Eric heard Zander, one of the restaurant's more recent hires, as he handed the check to some of his customers. "Thank you for dining with us for lunch today, it really is a pleasure seeing you again. By the way, we have started a loyalty program in appreciation of our customers, and I would like to invite you to join. As a "thank you" for becoming a member, we will email you a reward certificate for one of our specialty desserts next time you come in. The sign-up form is here with the check, and I can answer any questions you have. Thank you again – would you like me to get you another cup of coffee?"

Zander left the check presenter with these customers and moved to another table. When he returned for payment, one of the women at the table engaged him in some conversation about the confidentiality of her email. Zander's response satisfied her, because both of the women completed the sign-up form.

By the end of the lunchtime rush, they had enrolled almost a dozen and a half members in the "Friends of Fish Club", most of them having come from Zander's and Paula's tables. Eric was elated and disappointed at the same time. He couldn't understand why anyone would pass on enrolling, yet he was pleased because he felt the first month's objective of 500 members was reachable. Of course, not every server was comfortable "selling" this program the first day and Eric didn't want to push too hard on the initial day of the program's introduction.

The loyalty program was being managed and administered by another company Eric had found through the Restaurant Association of Maryland (RAM). The YouGotMeals email marketing program was a RAM "endorsed program" and as a member of the Association, Eric saved considerably more than his cost of membership.

YouGotMeals would enter the sign-up forms they collected into a database secured and managed in compliance with the requirements of the CAN SPAM Act passed by Congress. Of course Fish Outta Water owned the data and had to approve all messages sent to its customers. Eric didn't have the database skills or the legal knowledge, so this was the first of many services he needed to begin a permission-based email loyalty program.

Soon after enrolling, the Friends of Fish Club member would receive a "Welcome Message" from the restaurant. The purpose of this introductory email was to "welcome" the customer to the club, confirm her desire to participate, reward her with the first gift, and provide reassurance that her email would not be shared or provided to anyone else.

Creation of all the emails, including graphics, copywriting, links to the restaurant's website, and other "housekeeping" items, was all handled by YouGotMeals, allowing Eric to focus on the "20% of critical issues" that were within his capabilities and truly needed his hands-on attention.

A tentative calendar covering the next 12 months had also been created, providing structure and complementing the marketing plan that Eric and Dana had created for the restaurant. Aside from monthly email invitations to visit the restaurant, announcements of various promotions, and the ability to make reservations online directly from the email, Eric had also scheduled some free cooking classes available only to club members. Of course, "special occasion" emails would also be sent in advance of a customer's birthday and anniversary, inviting them to reserve a table (or the party room) and receive a special gift for allowing Fish Outta Water to share in the joy of the occasion.

Eric considered this permission-based email program critical and was disappointed that Dana had not started him on it 8 weeks ago when they had met. She explained that he needed to understand the big picture first and had to adjust his mindset regarding service, training, marketing, customer motivation, and priorities. She feared that if he began collecting customer information too soon, the data would sit and become stale, possibly resulting in customers who were turned off rather than impressed. Eric reluctantly agreed, as he remembered the numerous times he had dropped a business card with another restaurant or retailer, only to never hear from them or to receive some meaningless communication that was less than valueless.

The dinner crowd was growing as his 6:30 reservations arrived. It was going to be another busy night and he felt exhilarated over the progress he had made in such a short period of time.

At a table to his left, Mariana, another new server, was retrieving a customer's credit card for payment. He noticed that the party at Mariana's table was filling out their sign-up cards as well.

Permission versus Interruption Marketing

Per-mis-sion based e-mail: *n.* a low cost marketing medium providing direct communication with targeted customers and prospects, all of whom have requested information from you, or given you consent to maintain contact.

Seth Godin's book *Permission Marketing* was published in 1999 and became a bestseller. Its success is not surprising because it resounded with business people across industries, and even today it is necessary reading for far too many business owners still caught up in yesterday's antiquated marketing.

To understand the power of "permission marketing" it helps to first look at its opposite. How does most media attempt to convey an advertising or marketing message to you? It accomplishes this through interruption.

Network and much of cable TV interrupts programming with commercial messages.

Radio interrupts your music, news, talk or specialty interest shows with commercial messages.

Newspapers and magazines place advertising throughout their publications and structure articles so that you are forced to go from one page to another to complete your reading, where more ads are strategically placed to grab your attention.

Telemarketing is the ultimate form of "Interruption Marketing" and it became so intrusive, it took an act of

Congress and the creation of a National Registry, a DO NOT CALL list, to alleviate this problem for consumers.

Other examples include pop-up ads on your computer, mass coupons via mail or through supposed "newspapers" that are virtually all advertisements, spam email, and direct mail solicitations that far outnumber the mail I actually need or want.

We stopped the mail at our house during a vacation that lasted one week. When we returned and mail resumed, the accumulated mail was delivered in a large white bin. I counted 93 individual pieces of mail, as follows:

Description	Quantity
Interruption Advertising:	
Catalogs: Merchandise and Education	10
Charitable Solicitations	19
Political Party Solicitations	2
Local Merchants	14
Credit Card and Mortgage	4
Private School Open House	2
Coupons or Letters	10
Note: Coupon Mailer with 44 coupons	
Local Paper (free)	<u>1</u>
Total Interruption Advertising:	62
Permission Advertising:	
Auto, Insurance, Travel	4
Holiday Cards	4
Investment	3
Bills and Notices	11
Magazines	5
Kids Mail	<u>4</u>
Total Permission Advertising:	31
Total Pieces of Mail:	93

The ads and marketing pieces outnumbered the necessary mail by 2 to 1! How many of those "Interruption Marketing" pieces do you think had an impression on me?

Obtaining Permission to Market

You do not have a permission-based marketing program without a database of customers and prospects, all of who have given you the "okay" to communicate with them.

Although there are numerous opportunities to buy, rent, lease, trade, borrow or use someone else's "permission-based" list, your communications with people on these lists are most likely to be viewed as an unwelcome interruption.

There are no shortcuts to generating a list. You have to do this yourself. Fortunately, assuming yours is a restaurant worthy of its customers' trust and repeat business, this is not a significant hurdle.

You can collect email addresses through your website (if you have one), but most sign-ups will occur in the restaurant as a result of an employee politely asking a customer to join, or making him aware that you have a program.

> **There are no shortcuts to generating a list. You have to do this yourself.**

The sign-up form you create should ask for as little information as possible because you do not want to frighten customers away. As consumers ourselves, we are already worried about being on too many lists.

At a minimum, you need the customer's email address, first name, and birthday. When requesting "special occasion" information, such as a birthday or anniversary, ask only for the month and day, as the year is irrelevant to your purposes (unless you intend to be in the life insurance business in the near future). Asking the year of birth will decrease the customer sign-ups as many people consider this to be an intrusion, plus it creates a possible risk for increased vulnerability to identity theft. Unless your email program is specifically designed to include children, you should include language on the form that specifically states the program is for customers who are 18 years of age or older.

Some of my restaurant clients do ask for more information, such as full name, address and phone number, and provide space for comments. I typically recommend against asking for more information than you need to get permission from as many people as possible, as responses diminish with each additional data field after four fields. Remember, you can always obtain more detailed information later. Inviting your customers to update their profiles electronically works when accompanied by an appropriate reward.

Data Entry, Maintenance and Security

Imagine that on the same day, you requested information from two credit card processors. One responded to you within a few days and the other one, well, just did not respond at all. Shortly thereafter you went with the company that responded. Roughly three months go by and you receive a flyer in the mail from the second company. It is an impressive brochure and it says the right things. It just was not timely any longer, and frankly, you doubted that the "Excellent Customer Service!" touted in the brochure could possibly be accurate.

When your customer signs up for your program, timely and accurate data entry, along with your first email, is important. Too often, restaurateurs collect business cards and leave them in a box in the back office. They fully intend to sit down one day and create a database of these customers because they intuitively recognize the marketing benefits. But real life intrudes and the business cards slowly develop a cover of dust, or even worse, mold. It is not just the opportunity that was lost; it is also the negative opinion that has now formed in your customers' minds.

So – take the data entry seriously. Do it quickly and send your "Welcome Message" (to be discussed soon) within two weeks.

Your database requires ongoing maintenance. You should constantly generate new members for your email club. You also need to immediately remove those members who request that they be "removed" or "unsubscribed" from your list, or report your email as spam to their Internet Service Provider (ISP). Aside from being the necessary response in regard to customer service, it is now also required by law.

Your database should be securely maintained and protected. It is an important asset that has significant value to you, a potential buyer of your restaurant, and your competitors. Protecting the data means it will not be lost in the event of a critical hard drive crash on your computer, intentionally destroyed by an angry employee, or copied and taken by an Assistant Manager to his new employer.

I am a member of a large hotel chain's rewards program. I recently received an apology letter advising me that my customer information, including my stored credit card numbers, had unfortunately been on a backup tape that was "lost." Although they had advised my credit card company about the potential problem, they recommended that I carefully monitor my credit card statements.

I will stay with this hotel chain again, but my last few reservations have been at different, unaffiliated hotels. The lesson? You need to secure and protect this data.

Email Design: Graphics, Copywriting and "Housekeeping"

Graphic design, copywriting, and ad layout are tasks that many restaurateurs perform on their own. That is probably unfortunate. If you have training and skills in these areas go for it. If the results are good, continue on your own because you know your customers best. However, if you have doubts about your success or if you do not have the time to implement, monitor, and measure the results, consider a professional.

Many small business owners, and restaurateurs fit this category; they prefer to create marketing plans and advertising in-house because of the cost savings. The typical independent restaurateur with a few stores or less will find most advertising agencies to be priced out of his range. The sad part is that the restaurant's potential is not maximized as customers and prospects ignore their in-house marketing, and their competitor's marketing efforts are magnified in comparison.

Advertising works when it is appropriate, targeted, creative and inoffensive. The graphics and copywriting are critical in your attempts to influence the dining behavior of consumers who read your messages. As key components of emails that you send to members, they need to reinforce your brand message, not detract from the message.

What about creating and sending a restaurant newsletter via email? I do not believe a newsletter is as effective as an (electronic) invitation to your restaurant or notice of a promotion. The average amount of time a consumer spends looking at an email is under 20 seconds. A newsletter requires considerably more time and attention, and in this "limited attention-span" world that we live in, your message needs to make its point very quickly. Graphics are important because it stimulates the brain differently than the pure text in most newsletters.

Many restaurant managers write an interesting newsletter, and these should be available on your website with a link from the emails you send. This gives you three benefits: 1) an effective email that gets your point across quickly, 2) a more extensive newsletter for those customers inclined to read a more descriptive communication regarding your restaurant, and 3) additional web site exploration since customers may be prone to investigate the rest of your web site once they find themselves with more pages to explore.

Even professionals make errors in their copywriting, usually to our great amusement. If you are writing your own copy, check and double check for speelling and grammatical errors. (I did that purposely to see if you were paying attention!) Have others read your copy to ensure the written message has the exact meaning you wish to communicate. Day and date errors are more common than spelling errors because it takes verifying against a calendar to find the error, as opposed to recognition in your brain regarding a misspelled word.

Caution is advised regarding copy that can be controversial or offensive. You risk upsetting existing customers with a promotion that is at odds with your brand identity. I am on an email distribution list from a family restaurant I enjoy. The emails are humorous and well written. One email however I am sure crossed the line for many readers. The writer jokingly referred to the "secret ingredient" that made one of their entrees so tasty. The ingredient was identified as "heroin." Although immediately disclaimed as a joke, I imagine that some customers took serious exception to the gag.

Word selection affects reader interest, and good copywriters know how to substitute words for maximum effect. Invest in a book on copywriting; what you learn will pay off whether you write your own ads or you are asked to approve ads written for your restaurant.

"Housekeeping" refers to added capabilities and requirements of your email program. Among its many provisions, the CAN-SPAM Act requires that you promptly remove customer email addresses when requested to do so. Lack of compliance in this area will lead to spam complaints, putting both your email program and web site at risk, as well as potentially subject you to fines and lawsuits. An "unsubscribe" link is critical, and proper database management will ensure you provide top service and maintain legal compliance.

You should have a "Privacy Policy" that explains how and when you will use your customers' email addresses. This is a necessary "good business practice" and can save you from problems in the future.

Consider a "feedback" link in your email. Customer feedback is critical to improving your business and ensuring that good customers are not lost because of a bad meal or experience. Feedback or comment cards are a poor option because servers have been known to unexplainably "lose" comment cards that indicate dissatisfaction with the service. This may be shocking to many operators, and I am certain it is not happening in *your* restaurant, but do not be dismayed if the electronic feedback you receive is not quite as complimentary as the written feedback on your comment cards.

Word-of-mouth is a critical element of your marketing; it is extremely effective and not that expensive. The loyal customer who tells a friend about the joys of your restaurant, particularly the food, service and atmosphere, is to be treasured by you. Email facilitates the ability of this loyal customer to tell dozens of friends about the joys of your restaurant, simply by forwarding your email invitations and promotions to everyone in his electronic address book. You should encourage this "sharing with a friend" and provide a link to make these messages more personalized.

Is "Email" Really Critical?

This is the last of six principles in ENTRÉE Marketing[SM]. We started with two principles related to four walls marketing, making your restaurant "enticing" to customers and providing "near-perfect service." The third principle, "top-of-mind" promotes the creation of a marketing strategy, all of its element contributing to making your restaurant the one that your customers think of immediately. The concept of human motivation is explored with the fourth principle, "rewards," and demonstrates how reward and loyalty programs proliferate in everyday life. A familiar tenet of business, the 80-20 rule, and its application to marketing, operations, employees, quality control and decision making, is our fifth principle.

So why, with all the marketing and advertising options available, from traditional mass media, to the high technology world of the Internet and search engines, to the low technology option of flyers on windshields, do I include permission-based email as a guiding marketing principle for restaurateurs? The more cynical of you will smirk and offer the explanation that I recommend email marketing because my employer provides a full-service email-marketing program for restaurants. But your explanation of my rationale would be incorrect.

I believe strongly that permission-based email is a bridge for every restaurant that effectively and economically enables personalized, relevant, and desired communication to be sent to those customers that contribute to your success or whose lost business can cause your demise. Unlike other media, email marketing is affordable by every restaurant, independent or chain, and it should be the foundation of your marketing strategy going forward.

If you are a small, independently owned sandwich shop open only for breakfast and lunch, located in an office building, you have many options for spending your advertising dollars, but few make any sense for you. Your potential customers either work in the building or are occasional visitors to the building. What else makes sense after you place the "OPEN" sign on your front door during business hours? You can (and should) create a "loyalty card" that provides a free sandwich after the purchase of 10 sandwiches. You can print flyers and put them on the windshields of the cars in the parking lot, but this is just as likely to anger office tenants as much as bring them in, not to mention the animosity you will earn from the janitorial staff.

Email is your answer. Sign up customers when they come in for their morning coffee and muffin. Offer them an extra "punch" on their loyalty card as an incentive to join. Send weekly emails that list your daily sandwich and soup specials. If business is dead after 1:30 and you are obligated to stay open until 4:00 under the terms of your lease, drive traffic in the mid-afternoon with an ice cream break, promoted, of course, via email. Send birthday greetings to your email club members, and "sweeten" their day with a free birthday cookie from you.

What will this cost the small, independent restaurateur? If done correctly, either internally or with a professional email company that understands your business, it is the equivalent of a cup of espresso per email address per year.

On the other end of the spectrum are the giant national (and international) chains whose gross revenues rival the GNP of half the United Nations members. Why bother with email when your media mix already includes TV, radio, outdoor, newspaper ads and inserts, mass coupon mailers, and product placements in movies and video games? Add email because you need to start "farming" your customer base along with "hunting" for new customers. Add email so you can test advertising for new products very cost effectively, without risking millions on mass media programs that may not work. Add email because in this very competitive industry, customers who become friends show more loyalty.

What will this cost the giant restaurant chain? If done correctly, either internally or with a professional email company that understands your business, it is the equivalent of a cup of coffee per email address per year.

I'd like a decaf with a little cream and sugar, please.

> ➢ Permission-based email marketing focuses on growing an asset, your existing customer base, rather than hunting for new customers with more traditional and expensive media.
> ➢ Email marketing is effective because it breaks through the clutter. Rather than interrupting a customer or prospect and attempting to force your message into his consciousness, your email communications have been explicitly requested.
> ➢ Unlike most media, tracking the impact of email marketing is relatively simple. When used as a coupon or certificate that requires redemption, the proof is in the number of collected emails. Calculate the dollar value of the revenue associated with the person or party presenting the email. If used to create awareness, track the open rate, forwarding rate, and "clicks" back to your web site from the email.
> ➢ Appropriate for restaurants of all sizes, and complementary with all media plans, email marketing requires you to develop a database of willing customers. Knowing your customers, communicating with them quickly and inexpensively, and obtaining their loyalty are critical for your survival and success.
> ➢ The Internet is and will remain the driving technology for this and future generations. Email is the "killer application" on the Internet. Start using it or risk extinction.

Chapter 12

EGO BOOSTING MEDIA
VERSUS REVENUE
BOOSTING MEDIA

June 25, 8:12 AM

*I*t was an early morning start again but now that Eric's managers were developing so quickly he could modify his schedule and take off a few nights a week. One of his better servers, Shilo, had responded well to the challenges of management, thanks in large part to the training she obtained through the restaurant association. Another new manager, Vanya, had left her previous job at a chain restaurant nearby to join Fish Outta Water because she had been so impressed as a customer.

Two new servers, Cynthia and Tyler, were neck and neck in the number of new "Friends of Fish" email club members they were signing up. (Eric was giving an MP3 player to the server who added the most email members this quarter, and the quarter was coming to an end. The way it was going, Eric was leaning toward giving both of these star performers the reward.)

The other focus during this quarter was increasing after dinner beverage and dessert sales.

Servers received additional training on "gentle selling" and were motivated with prizes that included concert tickets, movie passes, and Restaurant Gift Certificates that could be used at numerous Association Member restaurants.

Revenue in after dinner beverage and desserts was up an astounding 54% compared with the previous quarter! Eric figured it was a combination of motivated servers, along with the realization that they had not done a good job in the past in this area at all, thereby leaving significant room for improvement. He shuddered when he thought of all the money he had "left on the table" in the past.

He was also trying something this month that was suggested to him by Bryan and Adam, the owners of "Lauren's Last Stop Café." He had met these restaurateurs at a Frederick County Restaurant Chapter meeting. They had implemented a program where their servers could "buy" a single dessert for any one of their tables every shift they worked. This caught on and accomplished three things: 1) tips were larger from the party receiving this "gift" from their server, earning Eric the appreciation of his servers, 2) offering one complimentary dessert for a party of four people frequently led to the order of at least one other dessert as well as coffee or tea orders, 3) customers were thanking the manager on the way out of the restaurant and complimenting the "great" service they had received.

There was a knock on his office door and it swung open to reveal Dana. She and Eric were meeting to evaluate their progress in implementing the ENTRÉE program, decide on two new items for the team to focus on in the upcoming quarter, do a preliminary review of the quarter that was ending, and finalize his media buys for the upcoming quarter.

Eric retrieved an overloaded folder from the filing cabinet. It was full of written proposals for everything from commercial spots on cable TV channels to advertisements on local movie screens.

Just over two and a half uninterrupted hours later they finished. ENTRÉE Marketing^{SM} was working; revenue was up, customer feedback was positive, and focusing on a few problem areas had solved many of Eric's previous operational problems.

In order to maintain the momentum and continue growing the database, signing customers up for the email program would remain a focus in the next quarter. In line with the revenue growth objective, extensive staff training on the restaurant's wine selection would be scheduled over three days next week. Eric wanted his staff to offer suggestions and opinions based on knowledge. "This is a delightful wine with the parmesan crusted trout", sounds much better than "Oh – a white wine? I like # 32! I used to drink it a lot in college."

As far as the review of the marketing they had tried, both agreed that it was too difficult to track the results of the local newspaper ads, and neither Eric nor Dana felt there was a big impact. One coupon mailer had brought some new customers in, and a majority of these customers signed up for the email program. Reaching them would now be easier and less expensive.

A proposal to increase the size of Eric's ad in the phone book directory was dismissed, and strong consideration was given to actually reducing the ad size! As Dana explained, "People use the directory to find a specific restaurant, not to randomly decide based on the size or color of an ad, which seafood restaurant to try. Your customers need your phone number to make a reservation, and that's when they pick up the phone directory or search for your website. If you want to make funds available to try different advertising, you need to cut back in some areas that are not bringing you customers. Remember the 80 – 20 Rule!" Reluctantly, Eric agreed.

In place of the newspaper ads, Eric would try advertising in a local movie theater (16 Giant Screens!) this quarter. The focus would be on dinner and movie combinations, and his private party room.

The email promotions for the next quarter were also finalized. July would be "Independence Month", celebrating Independence Day and honoring the nation's veterans. Gift Certificates would be provided to an organization that assisted recovering soldiers and their families.

August would be "Escape the Hot Days of Summer at Fish Outta Water" and one email club member would win a weekend stay at a hotel in Ocean City. Eric knew the owner of the hotel, he was a loyal customer, and they had bartered food for lodging with each other.

September would be "Back to School" and kids could eat free (from the kid's menu) with the purchase of *an adult entrée. It would be a nice "welcome back" after summer family vacations. Customers with grown kids could bring in the email promotion and a picture of their kids or grandchildren (they love showing those pictures to the servers!) and receive a $5 Gift Card for a future meal.*

The staff was preparing for the lunch crowd that would start arriving soon, and Eric needed to manage his staff. He and Dana scheduled a follow-up meeting about six weeks out.

Your Unique Marketing Needs

We make our marketing decisions from the safety and comfort of our business; they either work or do not work and life goes on. Rarely does someone suffer immediate consequences of poor marketing decisions beyond "I've called this meeting because we need to get our revenue up, any suggestions? Also – did we finish the donuts?" If advertising and marketing were treated as truly critical to your restaurant's health, and someone was truly accountable, things would change.

Would you make the same marketing decisions if your life depended on it? If you were marooned on an uninhabited island in the South Pacific (think Tom Hanks in Castaway), what would you do to attract the attention of potential rescuers?

One option is to wave your arms and jump up and down when you see a plane overhead or a boat in the distance. The other extreme could include elaborately designed and strategically placed "Help" and "SOS" messages throughout the island, along with pre-set camp fires you could run to and start on a moment's notice. It is the difference between hoping and waiting versus planning and optimizing opportunities as they arise.

Every restaurant's marketing plan is different, because their circumstances differ. Size, location, competition, access to capital, customer base, and skills are factors in creating, implementing and managing a marketing plan.

Although McDonald's and Burger King may have the resources to compete with similar marketing efforts on a national level, the local store-level marketing is critical to an operator's success. The franchisee/GM can hang on the coattails of the corporate plan, or he can use that as a jumpstart for his own store.

A multi-unit chain with density in a given market can consider, along with its four wall marketing efforts, some mass media. The keys are multi-units to share cost, minimal driving distance to the restaurant units for those who receive the message, and cost relative to other options.

Problems arise when decision makers lose track of reality, and this sometimes includes the outside experts you hire to help you! Advertising agencies may be more appropriate in assisting large national and regional chains, but they may have difficulty adding the necessary four walls marketing tactics to the media mix. Certainly not all agencies are guilty of this, but too many still lean toward mass media at the exclusion of more appropriate local and lower cost marketing options.

Piccadilly Pub, an established 14-unit chain in Massachusetts, worked with marketing consultant Rick

Hendrie to create a plan that focused on local marketing. The plan was presented to an advertising agency for recommendations, but the agency's proposal back to Piccadilly Pub was rejected. Instead of concentrating on the items identified in the marketing plan, the agency proposed a $250,000 buy of TV commercials throughout Massachusetts. The bulk of their marketing budget would be used in an extremely inefficient and ineffective way. Although $250,000 may seem like a lot to many independent restaurateurs, it buys very little TV commercial time. The result might have been good "reach", although not necessarily of people close enough to Piccadilly Pub locations. "Frequency" would be abandoned because there is just so much money available, and many restaurateurs are forced to choose between these objectives.

The agency plan was rejected and replaced by local advertising, including direct mail, some local newspaper ads, and the implementation of a loyalty club via email called the "Pic Pub Club." This plan cost a fraction of the proposed campaign and it is yielding strong results.

Ego versus Results

As a business owner myself, I have longed for the day when I could ask my friends if they saw my TV commercial, heard my clever jingle on the radio, or happened to run across my full page ad in a popular magazine. I imagined the excitement I would feel when my company's name was plastered across different mass media venues, friends would pat me on the back, and my kids would look up at me with the awe they used to when I pulled nickels out of their ears.

Unless I change industries, that day should never come. My current occupation and company is geared to provide services for the foodservice industry, its restaurants and suppliers. I undoubtedly would reach restaurant owners with a TV commercial for this book, but 99.7% of the viewers would have no interest in my thoughts on restaurant marketing.

The net result would be an ego boost with some sales, but the cost of the advertising would put me out of business.

Let us contrast the "ego media" approach with more targeted marketing. I could contact State Restaurant Associations and provide presentations on ENTRÉE Marketing^{SM}. I would send emails to all of my clients, prospects, and the thousands of people who have attended my presentations in the past. A targeted direct mail campaign to restaurant owners around the country could be implemented. There are numerous options, less glamorous than TV or radio, that would nevertheless provide me the sales and exposure I need.

General Recommendations

Now let us look at your marketing and see what media options might be appropriate.

Television: This is a great option for reaching large quantities of people. Skip it unless you are a giant in the industry or have a significant quantity of restaurants in a small number of markets. Although television is in everyone's home, commercials are having less impact than ever, despite their rising costs. Fewer people are watching because they have so many other options to entertain or inform them. More consumers are skipping commercials when watching recorded shows. This is why you see more and more product placement within the shows, thereby ensuring exposure. Think Coca Cola on *American Idol* or Apple Computers on *Sex in the City*.

I once visited a restaurant owner and learned that he focused on only two marketing approaches: 1) word-of-mouth, although I saw no evidence that it would necessarily be "positive" word-of-mouth, and 2) Cable TV commercials in the middle of the night. He was the "star" of these commercials, and I believe his efforts were geared more toward finding prospective dates.

Radio: Lower cost than TV, thereby enabling you to increase your frequency. It is still too expensive for most independent restaurateurs, although you can get very low cost radio time when nobody is listening. That is why it is so low cost.

If you have multiple stores in a given market and the cost is shared across the stores, it might be worth a try.

A better bet is to get a local radio personality to do his show from your restaurant or sports bar a few times a year. It may cost more, but it becomes a multi-hour commercial and your guests will talk about it for months afterwards.

Newspaper: Big city papers are very expensive and now want to sell you on their Internet listing of restaurants as well. (This shows where their readers are headed.) An occasional weekend guide could be useful, but you need to commit to a frequent schedule, and this takes the cost beyond many small independents.

Local or "free" subscription papers offer lower rates, but considerably fewer readers. Do not be fooled by inflated circulation numbers. The "free" papers that litter the driveways of our suburbs or are available in local stores are frequently unopened, especially when compared with "non-free" newspapers.

<u>Magazines</u>: National magazines are obviously a poor choice for local restaurants, although some clever restaurateurs have had some success by working with other similar restaurants in different markets. You will frequently see ads in Airline Magazines that highlight some of the "Finest Steak Houses in the Country," "or the "10 Best Seafood Restaurants in America." This is a potential way to reach and influence the traveling businessperson or tourist as he or she hurtles through the air in a metal tube with wings at 500 miles an hour.

Local magazines are an excellent source for reaching many readers and potential customers who are curious to try new restaurants. If you are not directly in the city but are located in the suburbs, ask the magazine about their sales, subscribers and distribution within 10 miles of your restaurant. The numbers may justify a test.

<u>Outdoor Billboards</u>: Prices are all over the map for outdoor advertising, with highway billboards priced out of reach for most restaurants, while highway directional signs are more affordable. The Cracker Barrel has developed a fantastic strategy of obtaining billboards near their stores (or do they only locate stores where they can get billboards close by?) that direct diners and their families to the restaurant. This is a great example of maximizing the Recency Theory, as these billboards reach tens of

thousands of consumers every day as meal times approach. I have never seen a Cracker Barrel TV commercial, which is not to say they do not advertise on TV, but I have probably seen their logo hundreds of times throughout my life while driving.

This is an area where the little guy can compete with the big guy in drawing attention to his restaurant, especially since Outdoor comes in many forms. You can advertise on the sides of payphone enclosures and direct people to your restaurant. You have bus shelters, park benches, even parking meter advertising in some markets, some of which may be viable for your restaurant.

<u>Phone Book Directories</u>: If your business is primarily local, you are probably fine with a simple listing, and you can bold it if you want extra attention. Think about the phone book and how it is used for restaurant searches. More often than not, it is a customer looking for a specific restaurant that he already knows. He finds the listing and either calls the restaurant or writes down the address.

Nobody I know chooses a good steak restaurant based on the size of an ad in the phone book.

If your restaurant customer base includes a great many tourists, you can enlarge the phone book ad, but do not get caught up in paying $200+ a month. Keep in mind your own experiences when traveling. If you are in a new city and want to find a restaurant, you will probably check the travel guide, full color restaurant guide in your room, or ask for a recommendation from a hotel staff member. Tourists randomly choose restaurants from the phone book as often as they read the Bible left in the dresser drawer.

Mass Coupon Mailers: This can be an effective way to build awareness of your restaurant among new prospects, plus you can easily track the results. Be careful not to overspend by buying mailings in areas beyond 10 miles that are already well serviced by local restaurants similar to yours.

Start by choosing zip codes within 3 miles of your restaurant and slowly expand to 5 miles out. If you are a legitimate destination restaurant, you can start with zip codes 10 miles out and expand further for a future mailing.

Always measure the response to ensure your ad is effective and that you are not searching for customers beyond your natural geographic base.

This strategy is also more effective for QSR, casual, and family restaurants. Higher end fine dining restaurants should consider a solo direct mail piece even though the cost is higher.

Public Relations: This can be an expensive option for many independent restaurateurs, but if your restaurant is truly exceptional in many ways, it may be worth a short-term investment. Typically, PR should be in place before you first open so it drives traffic to your restaurant early on, enabling you to cement the relationship with your food, service, loyalty, and email program.

If you have multiple stores and/or are relatively high end, maintaining awareness of your brand in the local papers or on the local news channels is an effective strategy.

Want a cheap alternative to a PR professional? If you have the facilities, offer to host private luncheons for your local Chamber of Commerce Meetings, or various networking groups, at your restaurant. You can charge full price but donate a small percentage of the proceeds back to the hosting group to cover their administrative costs. You will get exposure among dozens to hundreds of businesspeople and community leaders, many of whom will become repeat customers.

Web Sites: More and more restaurants are adding web sites to their marketing mix, and you should as well. It is time – most of your customers have web access, and in many parts of the country, broadband is prevalent.

In the old days, web sites were the equivalent of phone book directories. An existing customer would go to your web site for your phone number, address, and directions.

Today your customers expect more. They want to see your menu so they can forward the web page to their friends. They are curious about your ability to handle private parties and what, if any, catering options do you offer. They want this information without having to first call your restaurant and speak with a receptionist who is best trained at taking reservations. Do you regularly provide entertainment? This is where they will check your schedule.

From your standpoint, your website is a 24 hour a day, 7 day a week salesperson that provides answers, enables reservations, and can reflect well on your brand. Plus, it is not affected by changes in the Minimum Wage Laws.

Be careful about signing up with someone who takes ownership of your "URL", the English language web address used to reach you. If your web designer or Internet Service Provider owns "www.yourrestaurantname.com", you may lose this valuable name if you change vendors.

Search Engine Marketing: Although your restaurant caters to a local crowd, it will receive "hits" from non-customers. This occurs as tourists check restaurants in advance of a scheduled trip, or businesspeople search for the location of a favored restaurant brand in a new city. You may also find your restaurant included in the directories of state tourist boards, or your restaurant association.

Permission-based Email: If you do not have a program, get started today. If you have started collecting names, use them before the database becomes stale and your customers stop caring about your failed efforts.

You need to maintain discipline in sending the emails on a regular, but not too frequent basis. The great majority of my clients send monthly emails and two extra special occasion emails, like birthday and anniversary, during the year.

Many of your customers look forward to these email invitations. They are relevant to their lifestyles, since they enjoy eating out. The emails are personalized, showing that you care enough not to address them as "Dear Valued Customer." (If they were so "valued", wouldn't you know their names?) Your customers learn to anticipate the messages as you get into a regular schedule. And unlike the great majority of all the advertising they are exposed to on a daily basis, your customers desire your messages.

August 13, 5:17 PM

*I*t *was fun to finally be on a family vacation again. The kids were enjoying the beach and the sports. They had met some nice families, one from Australia and the other from San Diego, and planning for future vacations was already underway.*

Eric was in touch with his managers at Fish Outta Water everyday. He wasn't worried; he was excited about the progress they had made in only 10 months!

Revenue and profits were up, and he was even accelerating his payments of the principal on his bank loans, much to the surprise of Jordan Adams. ("Are you sure you do not need me to increase your line of credit, Eric?" implored Jordan on the phone just last week. "Just like a banker," Eric thought. "He's there with the money when I no longer need it.")

It was time to think about dinner. "Any ideas for a good family restaurant?" asked Eric, turning to his side.

"Absolutely," answered Gene, the new friend from San Diego. "I know of a great place near here with a fun atmosphere we'll all enjoy. The food and service are exceptional. You may have seen their ad in the hotel directory, as a matter of fact! I happen to also be in their reward club, and I even have an email certificate for dessert for all of us."

ENTRÉE Marketing[SM] *strikes again!*

Life's short. Eat out more.

Mason Harris

APPENDIX A

Join Your Restaurant Association!

I am a strong believer in Trade Associations and I know from personal experience, many times over, how the efforts of Associations have benefited me, and others in my industry.

If you are a member of the National Restaurant Association or your State Association, I sincerely thank you. Your willingness to invest, and I strongly consider it to be a true "investment", shows a commitment to your industry, your restaurant, your career, and your personal success.

If you are not yet a member, please consider joining. If you become a member of your State Association, you also obtain membership in the National Restaurant Association. Both organizations work diligently to promote the restaurant industry. Their primary missions include educating restaurateurs, protecting you and your business from unnecessary and costly interference by regulatory authorities, as well as misguided groups pursuing their own agenda, regardless of its impact on others or limits on personal choice.

If not for the Restaurant Association of Maryland (RAM), and the New York State Restaurant Association (NYSRA) I would not have been in a position to write this book. Their belief in YouGotMeals and me opened the doors to numerous restaurateurs. These were your restaurant colleagues who generously shared their marketing concerns with me, helped educate me, and most importantly motivated the creation of the principles outlined in ENTRÉE Marketing^{SM}. In particular, thank your Marcia Harris and Paula Kreuzburg of RAM, and Rick Sampson, E. Charles "Chuck" Hunt, and Jackie Chin of NYSRA.

For information on the benefits of joining, educational and certification courses for restaurant employees, and the numerous programs available to members, contact information is provided below:

National Restaurant Association
1200 17th Street, NW
Washington, DC 20036
Phone: (202) 331-5900
Web site: www.restaurant.org

Alabama Restaurant Association
PO Box 241413
Montgomery, AL 36124-1413
Phone: (334) 244-1320
Web site: www.stayandplayalabama.com

Alaska Cabaret, Hotel, Restaurant & Retailers
Association (CHARR)
1111 E 80th Ave
Ste 3
Anchorage, AK 99518-3304
Phone: (907) 274-8133
Web site: www.alaskacharr.com

Arizona Restaurant & Hospitality Association
2400 N Central Ave
Ste 109
Phoenix, AZ 85004-1341
Phone: (602) 307-9134
Web site: www.azrestaurant.org

Arkansas Hospitality Association
PO Box 3866
Little Rock, AR 72203-3866
Phone: (501) 376-2323
Web site: www.arhospitality.org

California Restaurant Association
1011 10th St
Sacramento, CA 95814-3501
Phone: (916) 447-5793
Web site: www.calrest.org

Colorado Restaurant Association
430 E 7th Ave
Denver, CO 80203-3605
Phone: (303) 830-2972
Web site: www.coloradorestaurant.com

Connecticut Restaurant Association
100 Roscommon Dr
Suite 320
Middletown, CT 06457-1591
Phone: (860) 635-3334
Web site: www.ctrestaurant.org

Delaware Restaurant Association
PO Box 8004
Newark, DE 19714-8004
Phone: (866) 372-2545
Web site: www.dineoutdelaware.com

Restaurant Association of Metropolitan Washington
1200 17th St NW
Suite 100
Washington, DC 20036-3006
Phone: (202) 331-5990
Web site: www.ramw.org

Florida Restaurant Association
PO Box 1779
Tallahassee, FL 32302-1779
Phone: (850) 224-2250
Web site: www.flra.com

Georgia Restaurant Association
480 E Paces Ferry Rd NE
Suite 7
Atlanta, GA 30305-3324
Phone: (404) 467-9000
Web site: www.garestaurants.org

Hawaii Restaurant Association
1451 S King St
Suite 503
Honolulu, HI 96814-2513
Phone: (808) 944-9105
Web site: www.hawaiirestaurants.org

Idaho
Idaho Lodging & Restaurant Association
134 S 5th Street
Boise, ID 83702-5949
Phone: (208) 342-0777
Web site: www.idahohospitality.org

Illinois Restaurant Association
200 N Lasalle St
Ste 880
Chicago, IL 60601-1014
Phone: (312) 787-4000
Web site: www.illinoisrestaurants.org

Restaurant & Hospitality Association of Indiana
200 S Meridian St
Ste 350
Indianapolis, IN 46225-1055
Phone: (317) 673-4211
Web site: www.indianarestaurants.org

Iowa Restaurant Association
8525 Douglas Ave
Ste 47
Des Moines, IA 50322-2929
Phone: (515) 276-1454
Web site: www.iowahospitality.com

Kansas Restaurant & Hospitality Association
3500 N Rock Rd
Building 1300
Wichita, KS 67226-1341
Phone: (316) 267-8383
Web site: www.krha.org

Kentucky Restaurant Association
133 N Evergreen Rd
Suite 201
Louisville, KY 40243-1478
Phone: (502) 896-0464
Web site: www.kyra.org

Louisiana Restaurant Association
2700 N Arnoult Rd
Metairie, LA 70002-5916
Phone: (504) 454-2277
Web site: www.lra.org

Maine Restaurant Association
PO Box 5060
Augusta, ME 04332-5060
Phone: (207) 623-2178
Web site: www.mainerestaurant.com

Restaurant Association of Maryland
6301 Hillside Ct
Columbia, MD 21046-1048
Phone: (410) 290-6800
Web site: www.marylandrestaurants.com

Massachusetts Restaurant Association
333 Turnpike Rd Ste 102
Southborough Technology Park
Southborough, MA 01772-1755
Phone: (508) 303-9905
Web site: www.marestaurantassoc.org

Michigan Restaurant Association
225 W Washtenaw St
Lansing, MI 48933-1529
Phone: (517) 482-5244
Web site: www.michiganrestaurant.org

Minnesota Restaurant Association
305 Roselawn Ave E
Saint Paul, MN 55117-2031
Phone: (651) 778-2400
Web site: www.hospitalitymn.com

Mississippi Hospitality & Restaurant Association
130 Riverview Dr
Suite A
Flowood, MS 39232-8908
Phone: (601) 420-4210
Web site: www.msra.org

Missouri Restaurant Association
1810 Craig Rd
Ste 225
Saint Louis, MO 63146-4760
Phone: (314) 576-2777
Web site: www.morestaurants.org

Montana Restaurant Association
1645 Parkhill Dr
Ste 6
Billings, MT 59102-3066
Phone: (406) 256-1005
Web site: www.mtretail.com

Nebraska Restaurant Association & Hospitality
Education Foundation
1610 S 70th St
Suite 101
Lincoln, NE 68506-1565
Phone: (402) 488-3999
Web site: www.nebraska-dining.org

Nevada Restaurant Association
1500 E Tropicana Ave
Suite 114-A
Las Vegas, NV 89119-6514
Phone: 702-878-2313
Web site: www.nvrestaurants.com

New Hampshire Lodging & Restaurant Association
PO Box 1175
Concord, NH 03302-1175
Phone: (603) 228-9585
Web site: www.nhlra.com

New Jersey Restaurant Association
126 W State St
Trenton, NJ 08608-1102
Phone: (609) 599-3316
Web site: www.njra.org

New Mexico Restaurant Association
9201 Montgomery Blvd NE
Suite 602
Albuquerque, NM 87111-2468
Phone: (505) 343-9848
Web site: www.nmrestaurants.org

New York State Restaurant Association
409 New Karner Rd
Albany, NY 12205-3883
Phone: (518) 452-4222
Web site: www.nysra.org

North Carolina Restaurant Association
6036 Six Forks Rd
Raleigh, NC 27609-3899
Phone: (919) 844-0098
Web site: www.ncra.org

North Dakota State Hospitality Association
804 E Main Ave
Bismarck, ND 58501-4526
Phone: (701) 223-3313
Web site: www.ndhospitality.com

Ohio Restaurant Association
1525 Bethel Rd
Ste 301
Columbus, OH 43220-2054
Phone: (614) 442-3535
Web site: www.ohiorestaurant.org

Oklahoma Restaurant Association
3800 N Portland Ave
Oklahoma City, OK 73112-2994
Phone: (405) 942-8181
Web site: www.okrestaurants.com

Oregon Restaurant Association
8565 SW Salish Ln
Ste 120
Wilsonville, OR 97070-6901
Phone: (503) 682-4422
Web site: www.ora.org

Pennsylvania Restaurant Association
100 State St
Harrisburg, PA 17101-1024
Phone: (717) 232-4433
Web site: www.parestaurant.org

Puerto Rico Hotel & Tourism Association
954 Ave Ponce de Leon
Ste 702
San Juan, PR 00907-3646
Phone: (787) 725-2901
Web site: prhta.org

Rhode Island Hospitality & Tourism Association
832 Dyer Ave
Cranston, RI 02920-6714
Phone: (401) 223-1120
Web site: www.rihospitality.org

Hospitality Association of South Carolina
3612 Landmark Dr
Suite B
Columbia, SC 29204-4039
Phone: (803) 765-9000
Web site: www.schospitality.org

South Dakota Retailers Association Restaurant
Division
PO Box 638
Pierre, SD 57501-0638
Phone: (605) 224-5050
Web site: www.sdra.org

Tennessee Restaurant Association
PO Box 681207
Franklin, TN 37068-1207
Phone: (615) 771-7056
Web site: www.thetra.com

Texas Restaurant Association
PO Box 1429
Austin, TX 78767-1429
Phone: (512) 457-4100
Web site: www.restaurantville.com

United States Virgin Islands
Saint Thomas-Saint John Hotel & Tourism Association
PO Box 2300
St Thomas, VI 00803-0300
Phone: (340) 774-6835
Web site: sttstjhta.com

Utah Restaurant Association
420 E South Temple
#355
Salt Lake City, UT 84111-1319
Phone: (801) 322-0123
Web site: www.utahdineout.com

Vermont Lodging & Restaurant Association
13 Kilburn St
Burlington, VT 05401-4750
Phone: (802) 660-9001
Web site: www.vlra.com

Virginia Hospitality & Travel Association
2101 Libbie Ave
Richmond, VA 23230-2621
Phone: (804) 288-3065
Web site: www.vhta.org

Washington Restaurant Association
510 Plum St SE
Suite 200
Olympia, WA 98501-1587
Phone: (360) 956-7279
Web site: www.wrahome.com

West Virginia Hospitality and Travel Association
PO Box 2391
Charleston, WV 25328-2391
Phone: (304) 342-6511
Web site: www.wvhta.com

Wisconsin Restaurant Association
2801 Fish Hatchery Rd
Madison, WI 53713-3120
Phone: (608) 270-9950
Web site: www.wirestaurant.org

Wyoming Lodging & Restaurant Association
PO Box 1003
Cheyenne, WY 82003-1003
Phone: (307) 634-8816
Web site: www.wlra.org

ABOUT THE AUTHOR

Mason Harris is the President of Robin Technologies, Inc., and AdsOnTarget, Inc. His company introduced the YouGotMeals permission-based email marketing program for restaurants in 2003, and it now has clients nationally.

Mason grew up in New York City, where he learned the joy of bagels, delis, Little Italy and Chinatown – as both a customer and provider of service. He received his BA from Queens College – City University of New York, and his MBA in Marketing from the State University of New York (SUNY) at Buffalo.

His enthusiasm for educating restaurateurs is expressed in his speaking engagements, columns, and now this book. (Why not use Mason as a guest speaker for your next conference or seminar?)

Residing in Potomac, Maryland, with his family, and despite his wife's fantastic cooking, Mason loves to eat out.

He can be reached at mharris@yougotmeals.com.